THE LITTLE BIG CHEF

My First Kids Cookbook, 100 Fun and Easy Recipes

Written by © Don Preston

TABLE OF CONTENTS

INTRODUCTION 8

PART 1: EVERYDAY KITCHEN SKILLS AND COOKING GUIDE.................................. 10

CHAPTER 1: BASIC KITCHEN RULES.. 12

    THE LITTLE BIG SECRETS 13

    SAFETY TIPS FOR THE LITTLE BIG CHEF 16

    WHY YOU NEED TO KEEP A CLEAN KITCHEN 18

CHAPTER 2: PANTRY, REFRIGERATOR, AND FREEZER STAPLES 20

    BASIC PANTRY SEASONINGS 21

    BAKING ESSENTIALS 21

    SWEETENERS 22

    RICE AND GRAINS... 22

    SNACK AND CEREALS.. 22

    CANNED GOODS 23

    DRIED HERBS AND SPICES 23

    REFRIGERATOR ESSENTIALS 24

    FRESH PRODUCE 24

    CONDIMENTS 25

    FREEZER... 25

    ORGANIZING YOUR KITCHEN PANTRY.. 26

CHAPTER 3: TEACHING KNIFE SKILLS 28

    THE ANATOMY OF A CHEF`S KNIFE...30

    HOW TO USE A CHEF`S KNIFE 34

    WORK PLAN TO KNIFE MASTERY 36

CHAPTER 4: HOW TO SAUTE AND PON FRY 38

    GUIDE TO SAUTÉING 40

    GUIDE TO PAN FRYING 41

CHAPTER 5: BAKING AND COOKING WITH FROZEN FOODS 42

THE BASIC RULES OF BAKING 43

COOKING WITH FROZEN FOODS 46

PART 2: RECIPE SECTIONS 47

CHAPTER 6: BREAKFAST RECIPES 49

MAKING AN OMELETTE 50

SCRAMBLED EGG TOAST 52

BASIC PANCAKES 54

YODURT PARFAIT 56

RISE AND SHINE PARFAIT 58

PRINCESS TOAST 60

PBJ ON A STICK 62

YOGURT & HONEY FRUIT CUPS 64

FRUITY PEANUT BUTTER PITAS 66

FRESH STRAWBERRY BREAKFAST TACOS 68

GRILLED HUMMUS TURKEY SANDWICH 70

COPYCAT CHICKEN SALAD 72

TURKEY WAFFLEWICHES 74

PEANUT BUTTER OATMEAL 76

ROTISSERIE CHICKEN PANINI 78

LIFE-CHANGING SOFT SCRAMBLED EGGS 80

CHOCOLATE CHIP, PB & BANANA SANDWICHES 82

BACON BREAKFAST PIZZA 84

CHAPTER 7: APPETIZER & SNACK RECIPES 87

MARSHMALLOW FRUIT DIP 88

LOADED BAKED POTATO DIP 90

KIDDIE CRUNCH MIX 92

PEANUT BUTTER GRANOLA PINWHEELS 94

RANCH SNACK MIX 96

LEMON-APRICOT FRUIT POPS 98

GLAZED DOUGHNUT HOLES 100

GRANOLA TRAIL MIX 102

CHEDDAR CORN DOG MUFFINS 104

TEXAS TUMBLEWEEDS 106

CHAPTER 8: LUNCH RECIPES 109

TURKEY RANCH WRAPS 110

CHICKEN & BACON ROLL-UPS 112

CHEESY QUESADILLAS 114

BLT WRAPS 116

BBQ CHICKEN 118

MANGO MONDAY MEAT LOAF 120

CHEESE FRIES 122

LUNCH BOX PIZZAS 124

CREAMY CHICKEN ALFREDO 126

RAINBOW SPAGHETTI 128

SWEET AND SOUR CHICKEN 130

INDONESIAN CHICKEN SATAY 132

SPAGHETTI CUPCAKES 134

CHAPTER 9: DINNER RECIPES 137

CHICKEN AND PEA CASSEROLE 138

HAM, MACARONI, AND CHEESE CHOWDER 140

POTATO CHICKEN CASSEROLE 142

HAM BEAN SOUP 144

SKILLET PIZZA 146

PIZZA SOUP 148

CHILI MAC SUPPER 150

CREAMY BEEF NOODLES 152

GARLIC BREAD PIZZA SANDWICHES 154

FRUITY CHICKEN SALAD PITAS 156

GARLIC TOAST PIZZAS 158

CREAMY TUNA SKILLET 160

BACON GRILLED CHEESE 162

EASY KETO CHEESY BACON 164

CHICKEN PHILLY CHEESESTEAK 166

HOMEMADE HAM, TURKEY, AND CHEESE POCKETS 168

SOUTHERN SALMON STEW 170

CHICKEN MEATBALL SOUP 172

EASY HOMEMADE CHICKEN NOODLE SOUP 174

CHICKEN RICE SOUP 176

TRADITIONAL TUNA SALAD 178

EASY KOREAN BBQ MARINADE 180

CHAPTER 10: SIDE DISHES 183

MICRO HOT SAUERKRAUT CLUBS 184

BROCCOLI CHEESE SOUP 202

ROASTED ACORN SQUASH WITH PINE NUTS 186

BAKED HERB POTATOES 188

CHIVE AND ONION CHEESY POTATOES 190

BROCCOLI DELIGHT 192

CREAMED CORN 194

SPICY BBQ CORN 196

MICRO COOKED MUSHROOMS PATTIES 198

LASAGNA IN A MUG 200

CHAPTER 11: DRINK RECIPES 205

STRAWBERRY MILKSHAKE 206

LEMONADE FOR KIDS 208

ORANGE CREAMSICLE SMOOTHIES 210

CREAMY AND RICH WATERMELON SMOOTHIE............... 212

PEANUT BUTTER BANANA SMOOTHIES 214

NO SUGAR FROZEN STRAWBERRY LEMONADE 216

MANGO JULIUS MOCKTAIL 218

LOW-CALORIE BLUEBERRY SMOOTHIE 220

STRAWBERRY LIME SMOOTHIES 222

OREO MILKSHAKE 224

PUMPKIN PIE SMOOTHIES 226

EGG CREAM 228

CHAPTER 12: DESSERT RECIPES 231

MICROWAVE MINI CHOCOLATE CAKE 232

RASPBERRY ICE CREAM IN A BAG 234

NO-BAKE PEANUT BUTTER TREATS 236

BASIC VANILLA CAKE 238

EASY CAKE MIX BARS 240

BASIC BANANA MUFFINS 242

ROOT BEER FLOAT CAKE 244

FUDGY MINT COOKIES 246

CHOCOLATE LOVER'S PIZZA 248

PEANUT BUTTER KISS COOKIES 250

CHOCOLATE MILKSHAKE 252

INDIVIDUAL PUDDING DIRT CUPS 254

MINI BROWNIE BITES 256

APPLE MUFFINS WITH STRAWBERRIES 258

CONCLUSION 260

ABOUT THE AUTHOR 261

INDEX 262

INTRODUCTION

When my daughter turned 11 and my son was almost 7 years old, my wife secured a new position at work and took business trips for several years. Our sweet family always liked to experiment in the kitchen, but my wife was honestly the chef all along.

In retrospect, I spent a lot of time in the kitchen at my parents' restaurant when I was a kid, where I learned the basics about cooking. I was curious to get back to my roots and childhood passion.

Then during a family meeting, our daughter Lisa suggested she would cook during her mom's absence, and to do so, she aimed to learn to be a chef in our kitchen.

Since then, we haven't regretted that decision once. It turned out that not only did cooking together help the kids to gain culinary experience, but it also ushered in a new era in our relationship as a united, happy, healthy, and loving family. We bonded even more and spent more time together.

Now the children, tweens, and teens can prepare a delicious breakfast, lunch, brunch, snack, or dinner. They can also show off their amazing skills to their friends or relatives. When their dishes turn out well, it offers a sense of confidence and pride in themselves!

In the age of technology, cooking as a family is greatly needed to achieve more face time and authentic moments. Thus, this book contains the best recipes the children have learned to make. They're super accessible and approved by the main judges – the children, teens, and tweens. They range from the simplest to the more complex.

Specifically, you'll find child-safe cooking guides and helpful tips in this engaging and informative book. Children will be introduced to kitchen equipment, understanding cooking secrets, and they will uncover interesting facts about the foods they'll be using!

Besides family bonding and following directions, this book also increases kids' creative thinking. There was a time we were making a dish of potatoes and I told the children a little more about this product. I explained when and where they first appeared, their various uses, etc. The children liked it very much. As a result, we did it all the time. Every time we cooked together, I told them stories of diverse foods. We even made it a game!

I'll always remember the explosion of their emotions the first time they cooked a meal, and we sat down to dinner as a family. You could see the immense joy they felt at the fact that it was their little victory!

Likewise, I encourage you to walk this culinary path. I hope you and your family will enjoy our book. I'm positive that it'll help you start from cooking together to the point where your children can cook on their own. In addition to the practical benefits, it'll leave you with the fondest memories of spending time together in the kitchen.

Teach your children how to cook and become a dream team!

PART 1:

EVERYDAY KITCHEN SKILLS AND COOKING GUIDE

CHAPTER 1:
BASIC KITCHEN RULES

THE LITTLE BIG SECRETS

You could call them 10 Kitchen Commandments, or just good sense.

Whether out of joy, or necessity, or both, people the world over are suddenly spending a lot more time in their kitchens, many of them wishing that they'd had the opportunity to actually learn to cook. But like I said, you don't have to go to culinary school to become a successful cook, home or elsewhere (although culinary school certainly will teach you a handful of skills).

As a former culinary student and food writer, it is imperative to share some friendly cooking advice that I think is valuable for the little big chef who is currently getting acquainted with the kitchen.

Cooking is an apt metaphor for life. Cooking is not necessarily an art but has artistic elements. It involves science, but also the nebulous element of intuition. It requires participation of all of the senses, including the sixth. It's the journey and the destination, since the end product is something that hopefully provides enjoyment and nourishes you.

As encouragement from former culinary students, including myself, who have gone on to a number of roles, culinary or otherwise, consider these 10 rules "the starting points".

1. CLEAN AS YOU GO

This is near and dear to my heart.

A clean, well-maintained kitchen is not only aesthetically pleasing, but is also beneficial to your overall well-being.

The best way to ensure an ongoing positive energy approach to kitchen projects in your home is to ensure that your kitchen is always ready for cooking. The best way to ensure that your kitchen is always ready for cooking is to not leave the dishes dirty. The best way to not have to tackle a mountain of dishes at once is to clean as you go.

2. LEARN TECHNIQUES, NOT RECIPES

Obviously you should feel free to seek recipes for inspiration and to even follow them, but pay attention to recurring themes rather than trying to memorize long lists of ingredients and instructions. A proper sauté is a sauté whether you are cooking classic French, modern American, or neo-space-age Icelandic. Learn the technique, and the recipe will be easy.

3. SALT

If there's one thing that chefs really want you to know it is this. So much so that it is iterated and reiterated in so many different ways. Don't be afraid of salt. If you ever wonder why restaurant dishes taste so much more impactful than those you make at home, it's the fearlessness with which chefs approach the seasoning process. (PSA: not everyone responds the same way to sodium, so don't necessarily let the USDA scare you into submission.)

Season each component individually. Salt the liquid you're cooking in. Finish with a little more salt if it isn't quite popping. And as a close second in terms of encouragement:

4. TASTE

Don't be afraid to season to taste. Most people don't taste or add enough. "Taste taste taste." This also harkens back to point number two: recipes are just guidelines. You need to taste, and—write this one down—ADJUST. If you think something needs more salt, add it. If it needs more acid, add it. If it's too acidic, balance it out with some more richness. If it's not done, cook it a little more. Don't simply settle for "but that's what the recipe said..." Not all ingredients, tools, and equipment are made equal. Learn to trust your senses more than the recipe.

5. USE YOUR TOOLS, CORRECTLY

Get yourself a good chef's knife, paring knife, and bread knife. With good knives come good skills. A good cutting board. Buy a thermometer. This isn't to say that outfitting yourself with all the latest gadgets will make you an excellent cook, but having a good, basic set of knives and everyday kitchen tools will ensure that you can use your creativity for flavor rather than the prep process.

The verb "whisk" should invariably involve an actual whisk. Certain things require a serrated knife, often called a bread knife, to be sliced appropriately, e.g. bread, which Instagram tells me you are all totally baking right now. (Tomatoes also require a serrated knife, unless you have a razor sharp chef's knife.)

If a particular cut of meat should be cooked to 140 degrees, there is a magical way to determine when that is without guessing. Cooking should utilize some intuition, but absolutely needn't be haphazard, and having the correct tools on hand, used appropriately, can guide you.

6. STAY ORGANIZED

Prepare as much as you can before you begin a recipe. Read through the entire recipe before starting. Until you have established good habits, time management is one of the hardest things to learn in the process of learning how to cook. Professional chefs use the term "mise en place," which literally means "put in place," to refer to all of the prepped components they need readily available before they even begin cooking. You can set yourself up for success by being ready with everything you need for the entire process so that you don't find yourself in a (literal) high heat moment unprepared for the next step.

7. BROWN ONIONS, NOT GARLIC

This one's from me. Onions get sweeter as they get brown. Garlic gets bitter. Be suspicious of recipes that call for onions and minced garlic to be added at the same step. Garlic should go later, and even better, added as whole cloves that will infuse your dishes with the sweet perfume of garlic, but that will get removed before you serve a dish. Trust me on this one. Separate the sweet from the bitter? In the kitchen as in life.

8. MAKE MISTAKES AND LEARN FROM THEM

It's never too late to start over. Have humility. You would be a fool to think that the highest rated chefs in the world never made a mistake. What's important is learning from those mistakes and pressing forward.

Cooking takes practice. It's more a craft than an art. If you want to get good at this, even in the privacy of your own home, commit the time. Be willing to take risks. Apply the lessons you learn. Go a little out of your comfort zone. Do your dishes tonight and show up again tomorrow.

9. HAVE PATIENCE

"Let it rest." This is both a literal and a metaphorical tidbit. Cooked meats should rest before slicing. Pastries should cool for a moment in the pan before removal. You should forgive yourself for today's transgressions and approach tomorrow with a fresh outlook.

10. HAVE FUN

"MORE BUTTER." I mean, it's never the wrong answer.

SAFETY TIPS FOR THE LITTLE BIG CHEF

Understanding hazards in the space you're cooking in can help you and your family avoid cuts, burns, and a bout of food poisoning.

When cooking with sharp knives and intense heat, accidents are bound to happen in the kitchen. Here are some kitchen safety do's and don'ts to practice in your home.

1. WEAR SHOES.

Ever drop a knife? Imagine that falling onto your foot. Ouch! Wearing shoes while you cook is always recommended. Not only will the shoes protect you from a falling sharp object, but they will also protect you from kitchen mishaps such as broken glass and hot water or oil spills.

2. LEARN HOW TO EXTINGUISH A FIRE.

There are roughly 164,500 residential cooking fires in the United States each year. Cooking is the leading cause of fires and injuries that occur in our homes. Be sure to always have a fire extinguisher in your kitchen and know how to use it. It takes only seconds for a fire to get out of control. Learn about different types of fires such as grease and electric fires. Never put them out with water. Instead, your best bet to extinguish them is to use baking soda or a pan cover. Suffocating the fire by removing air is the best way to put out most fires. A fire inside your oven is best put out with an extinguisher, and a microwave fire can be put out by turning off the appliance and keeping the door closed.

3. LEARN HOW TO USE KNIVES.

Did you know that a dull knife is more likely to slip and cut you than a sharp knife? In CHAPTER 3, you will learn a lot more about kitchen knife safety and how to choose the appropriate knife for the task at hand. In other words, using a meat cleaver to slice strawberries isn't the best idea.

4. WEAR SAFE CLOTHING.

Do not wear long, baggy sleeves in the kitchen. Can you imagine your sleeve catching fire on a gas stove? The outcome could be scary. In general, tops with fitted sleeves or no sleeves work best. Also, avoid wearing anything flammable or synthetic; when overheated, these fabrics can melt onto your skin.

5. PREVENT BURNS.

Make sure when cooking that the handles of your pots and pans are turned inward. This will be safer than someone knocking into them resulting in your food flying out and burning you. Always have potholders or oven mitts close by when handling anything on the stove top or in the oven. Don't use wet potholders or dish rags because they will not keep the heat from burning your hands.

6. ALWAYS WASH YOUR HANDS.

You would think this is a given, but people forget. Don't forget. It's important to wash your hands in hot soapy water before and after cooking. Try to use paper towels to dry your hands afterward because if a dish towel touches any raw meats or juices it can lead to a bad case of food poisoning. Be sure to also clean all your surfaces and sinks which may have come into contact with any raw meats or juices.

7. ALWAYS STIR AND LIFT AWAY FROM YOU.

When lifting a lid on a pot, there is condensation on the top. When lifting it off toward you, the scalding condensation can drip onto your skin, causing burns. The same goes for stirring. Make sure you always stir away from your body. Afterall, you want to eat the spaghetti sauce, not get burned by it.

8. DON'T SET A HOT GLASS DISH ON A WET OR COLD SURFACE.

There's actually a lot of science behind this tip. Glass expands when it gets warm and shrinks when it cools down, which causes stress, resulting in combustion. The best place to set a glass lid is on top of a trivet, cutting board, or potholder.

9. DON'T USE METAL UTENSILS ON NONSTICK, TEFLON PANS.

Cooking with metal utensils on Teflon or non-stick pans can cause flaking or chipping of the Teflon. This can, in turn, mix toxic compounds into your food. A better solution: use wooden or plastic spoons. Always.

10. DON'T USE THE SAME CUTTING BOARD FOR RAW MEAT, FRUITS, AND VEGETABLES.

We all want to avoid washing extra dishes, but this is one area in which you shouldn't take shortcuts. Using the same cutting board for meats, fruits, and vegetables is a surefire way to get the whole family sick with salmonella poisoning. The FDA advises you use two separate cutting boards: one for raw meat, poultry, and seafood, and another for fresh fruits and vegetables. If you must use the same board, its safest to prepare your fruits and vegetables first, wash your cutting board thoroughly with soap and hot water, and then prepare your meats.

WHY YOU NEED TO KEEP A CLEAN KITCHEN

If your least favorite chore as a child was being forced to wash the dinner dishes, you may find the idea of cleaning your own kitchen to be wearisome, stressful, and unnecessary. Unfortunately, despite the appeal of ignoring small kitchen messes, a dirty kitchen is also an unsafe kitchen. Remember, a clean, well-maintained kitchen is not only aesthetically pleasing, but is also beneficial to your overall well-being.

HYGIENE

Failure to clean your kitchen may result in the spread of bacteria and germs, which can cause you and other household members to become ill. Not only should you regularly wash countertops, sweep your floors, and clean the dishes, but you should also sanitize work areas and kitchen utensils you use to prevent the spread of bacteria.

PESTS

Cockroaches, ants, mice, and rats are frequent visitors to dirty kitchens. Proper maintenance and regular cleaning of your kitchen will reduce the possibility of pests. Some pests, such as cockroaches, are extremely skilled at hiding behind clutter. This makes it imperative that you not only maintain clean countertops and floors, but that your cupboard space is neatly organized, as well.

EASE OF USE

A clean kitchen is an easy-to-use kitchen. One of the biggest reasons to maintain a clean, organized kitchen is that working in a kitchen is simpler when your appliances are put away, the dishes are washed, and the countertops are clean. If your kitchen is cluttered with dirty dishes and spills, it is both difficult and time-consuming to bake or cook around the mess.

MAINTENANCE

Regularly cleaning your kitchen not only offers an appealing look, but also helps maintain your appliances, cupboards, and floors. Residue and build-up from lack of cleaning can result in costly maintenance repairs, as well as a decrease in functionality of your appliances. Furthermore, failing to clean your floors and cupboards regularly may result in the need to replace them prematurely.

SAVES TIME

How many times have you started cooking and then had to stop because you couldn't find a utensil or an ingredient? You know it's there but where is it?!

Just think about how much time you waste whenever you stop and hunt for something you need. This is frustrating to say the least and could so easily be avoided if you had an organized kitchen.

Create zones for prepping, cooking, and cleaning up so that everything you need for a specific task is nearby and easy to find. This will definitely help you save time in the kitchen.

YOU'LL COOK MORE

I think the best benefit of having an organized kitchen is you'll actually want to get in there and cook. A tidy and clean kitchen is inviting and encourages you to use it.

When you cook often, you'll enjoy more nutritious and cheaper meals than ones you would buy. So, not only will you eat food that's better for you, you will also save money.

Have I convinced you about the rewards of having an organized kitchen yet? It doesn't matter if you have a tiny kitchen or a large one, they all benefit from good organization systems.

CHAPTER 2:
PANTRY, REFRIGERATOR, AND FREEZER STAPLES

I like to keep a well-stocked pantry, freezer, and refrigerator so that I can throw together a meal at a moment's notice. When life gets busy, it's nice to know I have what I need to cook a quick dinner if I can't get to the grocery store.

Let's not forget about the refrigerator and freezer! Make sure you have a good supply of cold essentials too. From essentials that you need to make a quick and easy protein, great for breakfast, lunch, and dinner to staples for baking or making creamy sauces and smoothies.

The foods you should always have in your pantry are common ones you'll find in many recipes and those that can form the base of an easy dinner.

Below is a list of pantry, refrigerator, and freezer staples you should always keep stocked to whip up a healthy meal without a trip to the grocery store.

BASIC PANTRY SEASONINGS

These are the most common spices called for in most recipes included in this book.

- Garlic powder
- Onion powder
- Garlic salt
- Cayenne pepper
- Chili powder
- Cumin
- Dried oregano
- Dried thyme
- Dried parsley
- Paprika
- Grill seasoning
- Red chili pepper flakes
- Cinnamon
- Nutmeg

BAKING ESSENTIALS

- Baking soda
- Baking powder
- Semi-sweet chocolate chips

- Flour
- Sugar
- Brown sugar
- Powdered sugar
- Cocoa powder
- Dried fruit/nuts
- Old fashioned oats
- Corn starch
- Yeast

SWEETENERS

- Granulated sugar
- Confectioners' sugar
- Brown sugar
- Maple syrup
- Honey
- Agave syrup

RICE AND GRAINS

- Long-grain white rice
- Brown rice
- Grains: bulgur, uinoa, couscous, or farro
- Pasta: standard, whole grain, rice noodles, or egg noodles
- Polenta
- Breadcrumbs: plain or panko

SNACK AND CEREALS

- Crackers
- Tortillas
- Cookies or biscuits
- Pretzels
- Marshmallows
- Popcorn kernels
- Dried fruit: raisins, apricots, or cherries

- Seeds: sunflower, flax, chia, or hemp
- Peanut butter or almond butter
- Applesauce
- Breakfast cereal
- Old-fashioned rolled oats

CANNED GOODS

- Chicken broth
- Beans: cannellini, navy, chickpeas, or black
- Vegetables: hominy, corn, or green beans
- Olives or capers
- Chiles: chipotles in adobo or pickled jalapenos
- Salsa
- Tomatoes
- Tomato paste
- Roasted red peppers
- Tuna
- Anchovy fillets or paste

DRIED HERBS AND SPICES

- Bay leaves
- Cajun seasoning
- Cayenne pepper
- Chili powder
- Crushed red pepper
- Curry powder
- Fennel or dill seed
- Granulated garlic
- Ground cinnamon
- Ground cloves
- Ground cumin
- Ground ginger
- Oregano

- Paprika: sweet and smoked
- Rosemary
- Sesame seeds
- Thyme
- Whole nutmeg

REFRIGERATOR ESSENTIALS

- Dairy and Eggs
- Milk
- Plain yogurt: regular or Greek
- Unsalted butter
- Cheddar or mozzarella
- Goat cheese
- Parmesan (wedge)
- Eggs

FRESH PRODUCE

- Apples
- Avocados
- Bananas
- Bell peppers
- Broccoli or cauliflower
- Carrots
- Celery
- Lemons
- Limes
- Leafy greens: spinach, kale, or chard
- Lettuce: romaine, Boston, or mixed greens
- Cilantro
- Flat-leaf parsley
- Thyme
- Scallions
- Garlic
- Ginger

- Potatoes: sweet, white, or new
- Onions
- Tomatoes: grape, cherry, or seasonal beefsteak

CONDIMENTS

- Jelly, jam, or preserves
- Ketchup
- Mayonnaise
- Mustard: Dijon or whole grain
- Pickles
- Hot sauce: Tabasco, Sriracha, or sambal
- Worcestershire sauce
- Soy sauce or tamari
- Asian fish sauce
- Toasted sesame oil

FREEZER

- Ground beef, ground turkey, or Italian sausage
- Boneless, skinless chicken breasts
- Bacon
- Bread: baguette or sandwich bread
- Vegetables: peas, chopped spinach, or corn
- Fruit: berries, peaches, or mangos
- Nuts: almonds, walnuts, or pecans
- Dough: pizza, pie, or puff pastry
- Vanilla ice cream

ORGANIZING YOUR KITCHEN PANTRY

Now that you have (or at least know) the right pantry and refrigerator essentials, it's time to talk about how to organize them.

It's one of the spots of highest traffic in your house. It's no wonder you cringe each time you open your pantry to reach for an ingredient. Make cleaning and organizing this kitchen workhorse a priority. The good news is that it can be a fast, relatively painless job if you take small, manageable steps.

Remember, a well-stocked and better-organized pantry will enable you to cook more spontaneously.

Follow these pantry organizing tips to make grocery shopping and meal prep a breeze. This will make it much easier for you to decide on your next meal.

Clean First and Organize Second

Here's how to clear the way. Begin by throwing things out. It feels great and alleviates a big part of the task. Start by grouping items in one of two piles. The first pile? Items to throw out - including products that are past their expiration dates, stale, or have been crushed. These items are no longer safe for your family to consume. The second pile includes items you've not used in the last nine months. If you haven't needed that Basmati rice in three-quarters of a year, you probably won't be reaching for it next week. If the food is still safe, donate it to your local food bank

Ready to organize? Here's our top tips on putting everything in its place.

Make Every Inch Count

The secret to an easy-to-use pantry is visibility. You should be able to see everything you have. Remove smaller items (such as spice bottles or small cans) and place them in a basket or in a door rack. Adding a riser shelf or Lazy Susan will double your pantry space and help you find things quicker. You can find great storage options at the Container Store.

Embrace FIFO

FIFO is the accounting term for 'First In, First Out' and it's a great idea not only for figures. When it comes to your pantry, place newer items in the back and use up older items first. You're less inclined to let good things go bad. It's also a good idea to keep a pad of paper and pen inside your pantry door. Simply jot down items that need replenishing. The next time you go to the store, your list will be right there.

Organize for You

No two families or pantries are alike. When arranging yours, think about what will work for your hungry crew. This may be stocking items by type (e.g. bottles, cans, bags), by family members (you, your kids, your pets), or by their purpose (e.g. snacks, sweets, ingredients). There is no right answer. Just find the way that works for you.

Keep It Up

Your pantry can get disorganized after some time. Always put items back in their appropriate spot, and get the whole family on board by keeping food accessible and visible. Twice a month make sure everything is clean and in its place so you don't have to spend hours organizing it again.

CHAPTER 3:
TEACHING KNIFE SKILLS

Using a knife is an important skill that can be fun and useful when approached in a safe manner.

Therefore, in this section, I am breaking down everything about kids' knife skills, including safety, what knives kids should be using, and age-appropriate knife skills.

Before we get started, there are a few tips that will make a big difference. First, let's discuss safety.

Safety is such a broad topic because there's so much that can happen in the kitchen, but you can follow these basic knife safety tips and then take the steps to create a workable station at home that is safe and fun for kids!

THE SHARPER THE KNIFE, THE BETTER.

This applies to older kids using a small pairing knife or a chef knife. Sharp knives need less force to cut than dull knives. This results in less damage to the food. Also, a dull knife slows you down, while a sharp knife makes the work easier.

ALWAYS HOLD KNIVES DOWN.

Just like with scissors, don't run with a knife, and always point the knife with the blade towards the ground. In case of any accidents, a knife wound to the foot or floor will be less detrimental than one in a different part of your body.

Don't keep knives in the sink. The sink is a dangerous spot because it is hard to see through water. Also, knives can rust when soaked in water, so simply hand wash them and then dry them to avoid rusting (and having to purchase new knives!). Running your knives through the dishwasher is a big no no, stick to hand washing.

THE ANATOMY OF A CHEF`S KNIFE

The chef's knife is probably a cook's most important tool. And given the amount of time it spends in your hand, it's definitely worth making sure you have a good one.

A lot of people suggest purchasing "the best knife you can afford." But that's not much help unless you know what makes one knife better than another. Otherwise, you're just buying the most expensive knife you can afford.

The best knives are forged from a single piece of steel that runs the entire length of the knife. Read on for a quick guide on the various parts of a chef's knife, what they do, and why they're important.

THE BLADE

The best chef's knives are made of high-carbon stainless steel, which is a very hard metal that keeps its edge for a long time and won't discolor or rust like ordinary carbon steel.

To be sure, knives made from ordinary carbon steel aren't necessarily inferior. Some chefs love them because the relatively softer metal makes them easier to sharpen. Of course, they go dull more easily, too.

Chef's knives are measured in inches, and lengths of 8" to 12" are common. A longer blade lets you make longer single-stroke cuts when slicing. The so-called "German" style chef's knife tends to have a more curved section at the front of the blade, good for chopping in an up-and-down "rocking" motion.

The "French" style is straighter, and more triangular, which is good for a "slicing" type of motion where the knife is drawn straight back toward you.

In this picture, we see the edge of a Japanese-style santoku knife. The hollow, beveled indentations ground into the blade are designed to create tiny pockets of air between the knife and the product being sliced, reducing friction and minimizing sticking.

THE HANDLE

Unless you're very unlucky, the part of a chef's knife you'll have the most contact with is the handle. So you'll want to make sure it's comfortable and fits your hand. It shouldn't feel slippery or cause you to have to grip excessively hard.

Chef's knife handles have traditionally been made of wood, but wooden handles present certain problems. For one, because wood is porous, knife handles made of wood can harbor bacteria that cause food-related illnesses. Many local health departments prohibit the use of wooden-handled knives in commercial foodservice.

Bacteria can also grow in the tiny cracks where the wood joins the steel or around the rivets. Wooden handles don't fare well in the dishwasher either, though to be fair, you shouldn't be running your knife through the dishwasher in the first place. Still, even soaking a knife can cause its wooden handle to warp or crack.

For these reasons, knives with plastic or rubber handles (as pictured above) are increasingly popular. Additionally, some handles are made from a composite material consisting of wood that has been treated with plastic resin. That gives them the traditional appearance of wood, which many people find appealing, while avoiding the sanitation concerns associated with wooden handles.

THE HEEL

The heel is the widest part of the knife, located at the rear of the blade where it meets the handle. This section of the cutting edge is used for chopping hard items like carrots, nuts, or even chicken bones.

Knives with longer blades produce greater leverage, thus generating greater cutting force at the heel of the blade. A heavier knife also increases cutting force, but it's more tiring to use, too.

THE TANG

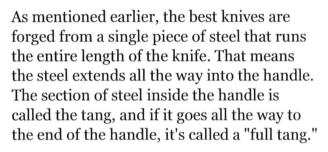

As mentioned earlier, the best knives are forged from a single piece of steel that runs the entire length of the knife. That means the steel extends all the way into the handle. The section of steel inside the handle is called the tang, and if it goes all the way to the end of the handle, it's called a "full tang."

In addition to providing strength, full-tang construction offers better balance, making a knife easier to use. "Partial-tang" or "half-tang" knives are barely worth talking about, let alone buying.

This picture shows the tang sandwiched between the two halves of the wooden handle. In knives with synthetic handles, the tang may not be visible.

THE RIVETS

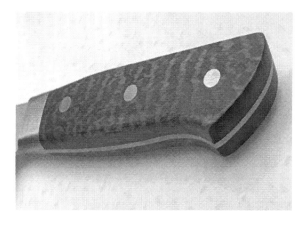

Rivets are the raised, cylindrical studs that keep the handle securely attached to the tang portion of the knife. This type of construction is typical of knives with wooden handles. If rivets are present, make sure that their tops are smooth and that they don't protrude from the handle at all.

In addition to showing the rivets, the photo above also shows the tang sandwiched between the two halves of the handle.

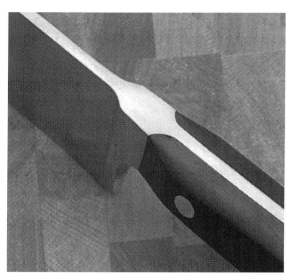

THE BOLSTER

The bolster is the thick shoulder of heavy steel located at the front of the handle where it meets the spine or the top (non-cutting) edge of the blade. In addition to balancing the knife, the bolster also helps keep your fingers from slipping while you work, thus preventing hand fatigue and blisters.

Not every chef's knife will have a bolster. A bolster indicates that a knife has been forged from a single chunk of steel, as opposed to being stamped out of a roll of sheet metal. These stamped knives are generally inferior to forged knives. The thickness of a bolster shows how thick the original chunk of steel was—and the thicker, the better.

HOW TO USE A CHEF`S KNIFE

Whether you are a novice cook or know your way around the kitchen, honing your knife skills is not only important for keeping you safe but will make your recipes that much better. Ingredients that are cut uniformly cook at the same rate and result in a dish that is cooked properly throughout. Since each piece of food is cut in the same fashion, the finished dish will have a nice presentation.

This tutorial will cover the correct way to hold a chef's knife as well as how to grip the food with your other hand to avoid cutting yourself.

PROPER CHEF'S KNIFE GRIP— OUTER VIEW

The photo below shows the appropriate way to grip a blade. Note how the index finger is wrapped fully around the blade. The index finger and thumb should be opposite each other on either side of the blade while the remaining three fingers are sort of loosely curled around the handle.

You should be gripping the knife mainly with the thumb and forefinger. If you find that you're tightly clutching the entire handle of the knife, just relax and loosen your hold. With practice, you'll get used to this grip, and soon any other grip will feel unnatural to you.

SECURE THE FOOD WITH THE GUIDING HAND

Now that your knife hand knows what to do, you need to make sure your other hand does as well. Your non-knife hand is called your "guiding hand," and its job is to hold the food to keep it from sliding around on the cutting board. This puts that hand in a uniquely dangerous position. With the knife blade quickly moving up and down, you need to keep those fingertips tucked safely away, while still being able to firmly hold the food.

The grip shown here is called the "claw grip"—by keeping the fingers curled inward and gripping the food with the fingernails, the fingers stay out of harm's way. The side of the knife blade should rest against the first knuckle of the guiding hand, helping keep the blade perpendicular to the cutting board.

ALTERNATE CLAW GRIP

In this modified version of the claw grip, the first knuckle of the guiding hand rests flat on the ingredient, with the fingers again curled inward safely. This time, the knife rests against the second knuckle rather than the first.

Both of these claw grips are acceptable, so use whichever one you feel comfortable with. You may want to start off with chopping an onion to practice getting comfortable with how to use a chef's knife.

WORK PLAN TO KNIFE MASTERY

START WITH:

BANANAS

Bananas are firm enough to provide some resistance, yet soft enough that a butter knife, or heck, a spoon, will slice right through them. They are long enough for a beginner to grasp, while still leaving plenty of room to cut the fruit into slices. Since they won't be uniform cuts at first, they are great to freeze for smoothies!

After bananas, move on to

AVOCADOS

A ripe avocado is smaller and a bit more slippery than a banana, but the soft fruit provides a similar cutting experience. This will help the child learn to curl their fingers under when holding the food to avoid cutting their fingers, yet the soft texture will still slice easily for relatively easy success.

THEN UPGRADE TO:

ZUCCHINI

The peel of the zucchini will up the challenge and the firmness of the vegetable will teach the child to either "saw" through it or to use the other hand to assist their chop. Again, this is great practice for keeping fingers out of the way while having a long food piece to grasp and practice on.

NEXT UP,

STRAWBERRIES

The small size of the berry will add a degree of difficulty, but the excitement of a true task (chopping off the green end) will prove to be motivating. Again, great practice for small foods and keeping fingers out of the way while using a relatively soft fruit.

LAST BUT NOT LEAST,

SWEET POTATO

It's best to assist by peeling the sweet potato and cutting it into long strips. However, the firm nature of the potato will require a more firm chop or the use of both hands. It's a great food to teach the "rocking" method of cutting and is probably the firmest food kid-friendly knives can handle before upgrading to the real thing.

Looking to get a younger child involved in the kitchen? Don't underestimate the versatility of the garlic press!

Both our children have loved playing with the garlic press since they were young toddlers. We began with the open/close variety.

You can let them cut a small piece of a soft food (avocado, banana, and cooked black beans all work well), then have them place it in the press and create "worms."

CHAPTER 4:
HOW TO SAUTE AND PON FRY

Cooking is thermodynamics. It's all about transferring heat. If you can transfer heat, you can cook.

A fast boil can kill a sauce and drive a vegetable to a limp death. Get too timid, and the hamburger goes gray and sauces never thicken. That makes dinner late and lousy.

There are deep, scientific reasons behind the magic that happens when heat is applied properly. It transforms the flavor and textures of beans and vegetables. It toasts and roasts and caramelizes sugars into dark and nutty deliciousness.

People spend lifetimes trying to master heat in the kitchen. But for most of us, simply trying to get good food on the table is enough.

To that end, having a strong game with a frying pan is a good way to improve your cooking. Sautéing and pan-frying are the most common forms of mastering heat in the kitchen. Learn them, and a world of recipes is open to you.

A few words before we start:

When you add food to your pan, it should always sizzle. If it doesn't, your pan is not hot enough!

Change the heat when you need to. Don't feel like you need to keep the pan over medium-high heat AT ALL TIMES just because a recipe says so. If things are browning too fast, turn the heat down. No noise or movement in the pan? Turn the heat up!

Not all stovetops are created equal, so keep an eye on yours and become used to its quirks and temperatures.

GUIDE TO SAUTÉING

To sauté means to cook small pieces of food over medium-high to high heat until browned on the outside and cooked through. Think of shrimp, cut vegetables, and meat that has been cut into small pieces. The term sauté comes from the French "to jump."

The jumping is of two types, one more important to the technique than the other. The jumping refers to the way the pieces of food appear to jump in the pan as the moisture is forced out by the high heat of the pan and oil.

Jump also refers to the very chef-ly manipulation of the pan, allowing the cook to toss the pieces a bit into the air so they cook evenly.

While that maneuver is impressive, it is not necessary to achieve a sauté since all it really does is make the food leave the cooking surface, and therefore slow down the cooking process a bit. For myself, I make sure that the food cooks evenly while I'm sautéing by moving the food around with a wooden spatula.

How to Sauté:

- Cut vegetables into even, bite-size pieces.
- Heat a skillet to medium-high heat.
- Add a small amount of oil.
- Add vegetables once the oil begins to simmer. They should sizzle in the pan.
- Add salt for taste.
- Toss or stir vegetables fre uently until tender and slightly brown.

Expert Tips:

- Add a splash of balsamic vinegar or lemon juice for new flavors.
- Experiment with different cooking oils like sesame oil, extra virgin olive oil, or clarified butter.

GUIDE TO PAN FRYING

A pan fry takes place at a little lower heat than a sauté does. This is because the food to be pan-fried such as chicken breasts, steak, pork chops, or fish fillets, is not cut into pieces before cooking.

Pan frying requires a lower heat so that the exterior of the food doesn't overcook while waiting for the interior of the food to cook.

You still use the same amount of oil – just enough to glaze the pan – but the temperature should be lower during a pan fry. It's important to note that the oil should always be hot enough to ensure that the moisture in the food can escape in the form of steam.

The force of the steam keeps the oil from soaking into the food. This is important, even if you're just talking about a little bit of oil.

How to Pan-Fry:

- Remove excess moisture from your meat, poultry, fish, or firm tofu.
- Season each side with salt and pepper.
- Heat a skillet over medium heat.
- Add enough oil to coat the bottom of the skillet.
- Place seasoned food into the pan and cook for 3 to 4 minutes on each side until done.

Expert Tips:

- Try this method with boneless chicken breasts, salmon fillets, or boneless pork chops.
- Pan-frying also works great with extra-firm tofu and your favorite herbs and spices.
- Get more flavor by adding sauces to pan-fried foods.
- After cooking, remove the excess oil from the pan and add your favorite sauce.
- Toss the food to coat evenly. Make sure to remove the food before the sauce burns.

CHAPTER 5:

BAKING AND COOKING WITH FROZEN FOODS

THE BASIC RULES OF BAKING

Great Bakers Are Not Born Great – They Are Made Great Through Skill and Practice.

You do not need to have a special gift or a magic touch to work wonders in the kitchen. The secret is practice, practice, practice!

Some people seem to be able to toss things together and achieve wonderful results. This is a skill they achieved through many years of cooking and baking.

It's a treat for me to watch children roll up their sleeves, measure flour, knead dough, and bake from scratch. When the final products come out of the oven smelling delicious, kid bakers are proud of what they've made and always happy to share it with friends, family, and me (thank you!).

Cultivating baking skills in beginner cooks means getting kids in the kitchen at a young age. As they grow and learn their way around the equipment, ingredients, and techniques, they will become more independent and confident — and they might just develop a love of baking that can last a lifetime.

It's worthwhile to establish a few all-ages guidelines for good kitchen habits from the get-go.

Below are basic skills every baker (in this case, kids) should know. Follow them to master the art of cracking every cake trick in the book.

1. Softening butter

Butter should be at room temperature before you start, to avoid the batter curdling. Speed up the butter softening process (without melting it to liquid in the microwave) by grating the stick into a bowl.

2. Melting the chocolate

Instead of having to finely chop your chocolate, get easy melts such as NESTLÉ BAKERS' CHOICE Choc Melts. The best method for melting is using a bain-marie, half filling a saucepan with water, bringing to a simmer, and placing the bowl of chocolate melts on top. Make sure the bowl doesn't touch the water (or it will overheat).

3. Creaming the butter and eggs

Add room temperature eggs to the butter one at a time, beating between each addition. This will ensure a fluffy, creamy consistency and means your cake will have a springy, even crumb.

4. Sifting the flour

The secret to a light sponge is to actually sift your flour three times. The higher you lift the flour above the bowl, the more you'll aerate it. Always use a large metal spoon to fold dry ingredients into wet – if you use a wooden spoon, the mixture will lose all its air.

5. Baking the cake

Always turn your oven on 20 minutes before baking cakes and check the rack is in the center of the oven to ensure even heat distribution. Conventional ovens are generally better for baking cakes, but if you must use a fan-forced oven, drop the temperature by 68°F to imitate a conventional oven.

6. Checking it's cooked

During baking, don't ever open the oven door during the first half of the cooking time! If your cake is over-browning, cover it loosely with foil. Test if the cake is done by inserting a skewer – if it comes out clean, it's ready.

7. Cooling the cake

Always leave cakes in the pan for 5 minutes before turning them out onto a wire rack to cool. You'll know it's ready to be turned out when you can see the sides coming away from the tin and it's springy to the touch.

8. Icing the cake

Always ice on a wire rack over a sheet of baking paper. Elevating the cake stops the icing pooling around the bottom. Using slightly warm icing on a cool cake is your best bet for getting a smooth finish.

9. Sifting cocoa

Decided to keep things simple by just dusting your cake with NESTLÉ BAKERS' CHOICE Cocoa instead of frosting it? Using a sieve to sift the cocoa will ensure you evenly distribute the powder and create a masterpiece. Baking for the kids? Place stencils on the top of the cake using baking paper before dusting to make fun shapes.

10. Making it wow

Making an impressive decoration for your cake, such as a chocolate collar, is well worth the effort. The trick?

Well, there is a plethora of great decorations you can do with little experience right from your own home. There are certain tools such as an angled icing spatula or wire cake cutter that will aid in creating perfect layers and smooth frosting.

First, you will need a store-bought cake that is as simple and versatile as possible. You will not want to invest much in it, since the real pièce de résistance will be the decoration. All you have to do at this point is decide on the flavour and the number of servings you need.

11. Cleaning the cake tins

If you've greased your cake pans with melted butter or spray oil before lining them with baking paper, you shouldn't experience too many issues. For burnt tins, use a non-abrasive scrubber or you will damage the non-stick coating. It's a good idea to place them in a warm oven for a few minutes after washing up to evaporate any moisture around the rolled edges of the tin.

12. Keeping baked goods fresher for longer

If your cake has not been cut or frosted, you can safely freeze it for up to 3 months (wrapped in plastic wrap). If you don't want to freeze it, frosting will protect it from air and moisture, keeping it fresh for up to 4 days. If you've cut a slice, spread icing onto the exposed sponge to keep it fresh.

COOKING WITH FROZEN FOODS

Frozen foods can play a helpful role in the kitchen — they're budget-friendly, long-lasting, and can help reduce food waste. What's more, some research shows frozen fruits and vegetables may actually hold in more nutrients compared to fresh produce since they are frozen at their peak freshness. Nutrient value decreases over time, meaning some fresh produce that had to travel a long distance to grocery store shelves might be less nutrient-dense than its frozen counterpart.

Also, another benefit of cooking with frozen food is that fantastic meal ideas can be crafted straight from the freezer. Once you've discovered how convenient your freezer can be, you'll be cooking directly from frozen, it's also really easy to manage portion sizes. Use only what needs to be cooked and pop any food you haven't used straight back in the freezer.

The selection of frozen food products that can be cooked directly from the freezer is continually expanding, making it easier than ever to whip up a quick, flavorsome dish. From frozen herbs that can be used to add extra flavour to a main ingredient such as beef or fish, to luxury frozen vegetables that can be added into a delicious stir fry, you'll never be short of great ingredients to cook frozen food and dish up some wonderful, fulfilling meals.

Moreover, it can help to reduce preparation time, which is key for serving up a meal quickly when everyone is hungry. We have a selection of dishes that will turn your family's frowns upside down in a matter of minutes.

What you you can cook from frozen:

- Chicken breasts
- Fish
- Mince
- Sausages
- Bakery goods
- Desserts
- Fruits and vegetables
- Prepared meals
- Pizza

PART 2:

RECIPE SECTIONS

This Page Is Intentionally Left Blank

CHAPTER 6:
BREAKFAST RECIPES

MAKING AN OMELETTE

Servings: 1

Prep time: 6 minutes

Total time: 6 minutes

Never fear! Making an omelette at home is not difficult. With a few basic steps and a flip of the wrist you can pull this off in minutes. Fill it with whatever you have on hand—it's a great way to use up leftovers!

Ingredients

- 2 large eggs
- 1 tablespoon unsalted butter
- 2 tablespoons grated cheese, any kind
- 3 to 4 cherry tomatoes, cut in half and sprinkled lightly with salt
- 2 tablespoons chopped basil, parsley, or herbs of your choice

Instructions

1. In a bowl, beat the eggs with a fork.
2. In an 8-inch nonstick skillet over medium-low heat, melt the butter.
3. Add the eggs to the skillet and cook without stirring until the edges begin to set.
4. With a silicone spatula, push the edges toward the center of the pan and tilt the pan so the uncooked eggs move to the edge.
5. Repeat until the eggs are somewhat set but still a little soft in the center, about 6 minutes
6. Place the cheese, tomatoes, and herbs in a line down the center of the omelette.
7. Cook for about 1 minute longer, or until the eggs are mostly set but still a little soft in the center.
8. Slide the spatula around one side of the omelette at the edge to loosen it.
9. Slip it under the eggs, and use it to carefully fold the omelette in half.
10. Slide the spatula under the folded omelette to loosen it from the pan.
11. Tilt the pan over a plate and use the spatula to nudge it onto the plate.

Nutritional value (per serving)

- Calories: 221
- Fat: 17g
- Protein: 14g
- Carbs: 1g

SCRAMBLED EGG TOAST

Servings: 1

Prep time: 5 minutes

Total time: 13 minutes

This Scrambled Egg Toast is so easy to make, and so incredibly tasty, that it is going to make your morning better. Guaranteed.

Ingredients

- 2 slices of bread
- ½ tbsp butter, plus more to butter the bread
- 2 eggs
- 1/3 cup good quality feta cheese crumbles
- chopped parsley or dill to garnish

Instructions

1. Spread a thin layer of softened butter on both sides of the bread.
2. Fry the bread over medium heat for about 2 minutes on each side, until a golden crust forms.
3. Remove the bread from the frying pan and add 1/2 tbsp of butter.
4. Add the eggs and feta cheese and cook, stirring often, for about 3-4 minutes.
5. Divide the eggs between the bread slices and sprinkle them with freshly chopped dill or parsley.
6. Make yourself a cup of coffee and enjoy The Best Scrambled Egg Toast.

Nutritional value (per serving)

- Calories: 370
- Fat: 15g
- Protein: 6.5g
- Carbs: 41g

BASIC PANCAKES

Servings: 8

Prep time: 5 minutes

Total time: 15 minutes

Nothing says "weekend" like homemade pancakes for breakfast. This easy recipe will help you whip them up in less than 20 minutes.

Ingredients

- 1 ½ cup flour
- 3 teaspoons baking powder
- 1 tablespoon sugar
- ½ teaspoon salt
- ½ teaspoon vanilla
- 2 teaspoons butter (melted)
- 1 ¼ cup milk
- 1 egg

Instructions

1. In a large mixing bowl, add all dry ingredients (flour, baking powder, sugar, and salt).
2. Hollow out a place in the center of the dry ingredients.
3. Melt butter in a microwave-safe container (set at low power for 20 seconds)
4. Pour the butter, milk, egg, and vanilla in the center of the dry ingredients.
5. Using an electric mixer, with adult supervision, mix on low until all ingredients are well combined.
6. Use a spoon to scrape the remaining flour from the side of the bowl.
7. Spray the griddle with cooking spray. Preheat an electric griddle to 300 F.
8. For a stovetop griddle use medium-high heat.
9. Fill a ladle half full with batter and slowly pour it on the griddle. Repeat, leaving plenty of space.
10. When pancakes are filled with small bubbles, gently slide a spatula under the pancake and flip.
11. Cook for another 30 to 45 seconds and use a spatula to lift the pancake off the griddle.
12. Serve the pancakes with your choice of whipped cream, strawberries, blueberries, bananas, chocolate sauce, maple syrup, or butter.
13. Enjoy!

Nutritional value (per serving)

- Calories: 130
- Fat: 6g
- Protein: 5g
- Carbs: 14g

YODURT PARFAIT

Servings: 2

Prep time: 10 minutes

Total time: 10 minutes

I can never have enough berries in my life! I am a total fruit and vegetable lover. Add in all your favorite berries and infuse your mouth with this rich, thick and creamy yogurt parfait.

Ingredients:

- 2 cups vanilla yogurt
- 1 cup granola
- 8 blackberries or raspberries

Instructions

1. In a large glass, layer 1 cup yogurt, ½ cup granola, and 4 berries.
2. Repeat layers.

Nutritional value (per serving)

- Calories: 515
- Fat: 18g
- Protein: 21g
- Carbs: 68g

RISE AND SHINE PARFAIT

Servings: 4

Prep time: 15 minutes

Total time: 15 minutes

Start your day with a smile. This fruit, yogurt and granola parfait is so easy to make. If you like, use whatever favorite fresh fruits are in season and are looking best at the supermarket.

Ingredients:

- 4 cups fat-free vanilla yogurt
- 2 medium peaches, chopped
- 2 cups fresh blackberries
- 1/2 cup granola without raisins or Kashi Go Lean Crunch cereal

Instructions

1. Layer half the yogurt, peaches, blackberries, and granola into 4 parfait glasses.
2. Repeat layers.

Nutritional value (per serving)

- Calories: 259
- Fat: 3g
- Protein: 13g
- Carbs: 48g

PRINCESS TOAST

Servings: 6

Prep time: 10 minutes

Total Time: 10 minutes

Have you seen the vitamin commercial where two adorable little girls serve their mom princess toast? The princess toast actress in the commercial says "I have no idea what's in princess toast" – but we do! Taste this reipe and you will, too.

Ingredients

- 6 slices of white bread, toasted
- 6 tablespoons seedless strawberry jam
- 1½ cups buttercream frosting
- 6 tablespoons of sprinkles
- 6 teaspoons of silver or gold edible glitter

Instructions

1. Spread jam over toast.
2. Top with buttercream, sprinkles, and edible glitter.
3. Leave toasts whole or cut into shapes.

Nutritional value (per serving)

- Calories: 465
- Fat: 13g
- Protein: 3g
- Carbs: 82g

PBJ ON A STICK

Servings: 4

Prep time: 10 minutes

Total time: 10 minutes

Loves PB & J, yet hates the crust, or you are just sick of making it. Try something like this PB & J on a stick! How cute, fun and super easy!

Ingredients:

- 2 peanut butter and jelly sandwiches
- 4 wooden skewers (5 to 6 inches)
- 1 cup seedless red or green grapes
- 1 small banana, sliced

Instructions

1. Cut sandwiches into 1-in. squares.
2. Alternately thread grapes, sandwich squares, and banana slices onto each skewer.
3. Serve immediately.

Nutritional value (per serving)

- Calories: 415
- Fat: 14g
- Protein: 13g
- Carbs: 63g

YOGURT & HONEY FRUIT CUPS

Servings: 6

Prep time: 10 minutes

Total time: 10 minutes

This tasty combo of fresh fruit and creamy orange-kissed yogurt is guaranteed to disappear fast from your breakfast table.

Ingredients:

- 4½ cups cut-up fresh fruit (pears, apples, bananas, grapes, etc.)
- 3/4 cup mandarin orange, vanilla, or lemon yogurt
- 1 tablespoon honey
- 1/2 teaspoon grated orange zest
- 1/4 teaspoon almond extract

Instructions

1. Divide fruit among 6 individual serving bowls.
2. Combine the yogurt, honey, orange zest, and almond extract; spoon over the fruit.

Nutritional value (per serving)

- Calories: 97
- Fat: 0g
- Protein: 2g
- Carbs: 23g

FRUITY PEANUT BUTTER PITAS

Servings: 2

Prep time: 5 minutes

Total time: 5 minutes

Not only are these sandwiches delicious, but they're also healthy! Both big and little kids can help to fill in the pitas.

Ingredients:

- 1/4 cup peanut butter
- 1/8 teaspoon each ground allspice, cinnamon, and nutmeg
- 2 whole wheat pita pocket halves
- 1/2 medium apple, thinly sliced
- 1/2 medium firm banana, sliced

Instructions

1. In a small bowl, blend the peanut butter, allspice, cinnamon, and nutmeg.
2. Spread inside pita bread halves
3. Fill with apple and banana slices.

Nutritional value (per serving)

- Calories: 324
- Fat: 17g
- Protein: 12g
- Carbs: 36g

FRESH STRAWBERRY BREAKFAST TACOS

Servings: 6

Prep time: 15 minutes

Total time: 30 minutes

When our son was growing up, this was one of his favorite breakfasts. I've used low-fat ingredients in the past with good results, too.

Ingredients:

- 2 tablespoons butter
- 6 flour tortillas (6 inches)
- 1/3 cup cream cheese, softened
- 1 tablespoon honey
- 1/2 teaspoon ground cinnamon
- 1/3 cup vanilla yogurt
- 1¾ cups quartered fresh strawberries

Instructions

1. In a large skillet, heat 1 teaspoon butter over medium-low heat.
2. Add 1 tortilla; cook each side until light golden, 1-2 minutes.
3. Transfer to wire rack. Repeat with remaining butter and tortillas.
4. Beat together cream cheese, honey, and cinnamon; slowly mix in yogurt until blended.
5. Spread tortillas with cream cheese mixture; top with strawberries.

Nutritional value (per serving)

- Calories: 225
- Fat: 12g
- Protein: 4g
- Carbs: 25g

GRILLED HUMMUS TURKEY SANDWICH

Servings: 2

Prep time: 5 minutes

Total time: 15 minutes

A beautiful and vibrant beet hummus is the star of this healthy turkey sandwich. Beets are loaded with a variety of nutrients and fibers that can help lower blood pressure in just a couple of hours, fight inflammation and cancer, and can help boost your immune system.

The turkey loads you up with even more lean-meat protein, while the tomatoes add a nice healthy dose of vitamin C, D, and folic acid.

The feta cheese is a great source of calcium and the baby kale sprouts are a superfood that help boost your brain power with the greens' high level of folate. And although the bread's probably not that good for you, it helps keep everything together and it makes it taste even better.

Ingredients:

- 1/2 cup hummus
- 4 slices whole wheat bread
- 4 ounces thinly sliced deli turkey
- 4 slices tomato
- 2 slices Pepper Jack cheese
- 4 teaspoons butter, softened

Instructions

1. Spread hummus on 2 bread slices
2. Top with turkey, tomato, cheese, and remaining bread.
3. Spread outsides of sandwiches with butter.
4. In a large skillet, toast sandwiches over medium heat until golden brown and cheese is melted, 2-3 minutes per side.

Health tip:

1. Cut saturated fat in half by omitting the butter and browning the sandwich in nonstick cooking spray instead.

Nutritional value (per serving)

- Calories: 458
- Fat: 23g
- Protein: 28g
- Carbs: 36g

COPYCAT CHICKEN SALAD

Servings: 2

Prep time: 7 minutes

Total time: 20 minutes

Want a low-carb version?

If you'd rather ditch the extra carbs and go bread-less, try picking up some Bibb lettuce (or Living lettuce) and serving this chicken salad up in lettuce cups!

Ingredients:

- 1/2 cup reduced fat mayonnaise
- 1/3 cup sweet pickle relish
- 1/3 cup finely chopped celery
- 1/2 teaspoon sugar
- 1/4 teaspoon salt
- 1/4 teaspoon pepper
- 1 hard-boiled large egg, cooled and minced
- 2 cups chopped cooked chicken breast
- 4 slices whole wheat bread, toasted
- 2 romaine leaves

Instructions

1. Mix the first 7 ingredients; stir in chicken.
2. Line 2 slices of toast with lettuce.
3. Top with chicken salad and remaining toast.

Test Kitchen tips

1. Double the chicken mixture for lunch during the week—use as a sandwich filling, serve over salad greens or spread it on crackers.
2. If you're cooking your own bird for this recipe, you'll need roughly half a pound of raw chicken for every cup of chopped cooked breast meat.

Nutritional value (per serving)

- Calories: 651
- Fat: 29g
- Protein: 51g
- Carbs: 45g

TURKEY WAFFLEWICHES

Servings: 4

Prep time: 10 minutes

Total time: 15 minutes

Who knew sandwiches could be so fun? My family adored this medley with its fantastic taste and whimsical touch. It reminded me a bit of a homemade McGriddle!

Ingredients:

- 3 ounces cream cheese, softened
- 1/4 cup whole-berry cranberry sauce
- 1 tablespoon maple pancake syrup
- 1/4 teaspoon pepper
- 8 slices white bread
- 3/4 pound sliced deli turkey
- 2 tablespoons butter, softened

Instructions

1. In a small bowl, beat the cream cheese, cranberry sauce, syrup, and pepper until combined.
2. Spread over 4 slices of bread; top with turkey and remaining bread.
3. Spread butter over both sides of sandwiches.
4. Bake in a preheated waffle iron or indoor grill according to manufacturer's directions until golden brown, 2-3 minutes.

Nutritional value (per serving)

- Calories: 407
- Fat: 17g
- Protein: 23g
- Carbs: 41g

PEANUT BUTTER OATMEAL

Servings: 2

Prep time: 5 minutes

Total time: 15 minutes

Peanut butter oatmeal bowl. A satisfying 15 minute healthy breakfast that is wholesome, packed with nutrients and so yummy! Topped with fresh fruit, coconut shreds, and dark chocolate – a vegan and gluten free friendly breakfast!

Ingredients:

- 2 cups water
- 1/8 teaspoon salt
- 1 cup old-fashioned oats
- 2 tablespoons creamy peanut butter
- 2 tablespoons honey
- 2 teaspoons ground flaxseed
- 1/2 to 1 teaspoon ground cinnamon
- Chopped apple, optional

Instructions

1. In a small saucepan, bring water and salt to a boil.
2. Stir in oats; cook 5 minutes over medium heat, stirring occasionally.
3. Transfer oatmeal to 2 bowls
4. In each bowl, stir half each of peanut butter, honey, flaxseed, cinnamon, and, if desired, apple.
5. Serve immediately.

Nutritional value (per serving)

- Calories: 323
- Fat: 12g
- Protein: 11g
- Carbs: 49g

ROTISSERIE CHICKEN PANINI

Servings: 2

Prep time: 8 minutes

Total time: 20 minutes

This ooey-gooey, melty delight is packed with bacon, chicken, cheese and just enough lemon to tickle your taste buds. Other chicken panini recipes don't compare.

Ingredients:

- 3 tablespoons mayonnaise
- 4½ teaspoons grated Parmesan cheese
- 1 teaspoon lemon juice
- 1/2 teaspoon prepared pesto
- 1/4 teaspoon grated lemon zest
- Dash of pepper
- 4 slices sourdough bread
- 1/4 pound sliced rotisserie chicken
- 4 slices ready-to-serve fully cooked bacon
- 2 slices smoked part-skim mozzarella cheese
- 2 slices red onion, separated into rings
- 4 slices tomato
- 2 tablespoons butter, melted

Instructions

1. In a small bowl, combine the first six ingredients.
2. Spread half over two bread slices.
3. Layer with chicken, bacon, mozzarella cheese, onion, and tomato.
4. Spread remaining mayonnaise mixture over remaining bread slices; place over top.
5. Brush outsides of sandwiches with butter.
6. Cook on a panini maker or indoor grill until bread is browned and cheese is melted, 3-4 minutes.

Test kitchen tips

1. Go for freshly squeezed lemon juice when preparing this summery sandwich. Bottled lemon juice, which is from concentrate, won't provide the same bright, fresh flavor. Buy some lemons to get the job done.

Nutritional value (per serving)

- Calories: 653
- Fat: 42g
- Protein: 28g
- Carbs: 40g

LIFE-CHANGING SOFT SCRAMBLED EGGS

Servings: 2

Prep time: 5 minutes

Total time: 5 minutes

These ACTUALLY changed my life. I used to not be able to stand scrambled eggs. But boyyy I'm eating these as we speak and gosh darn they are amazing!! So creamy. So tasty.

Ingredients:

- 4 eggs
- 1/2 tablespoon butter
- salt to taste

Instructions

1. Melt the butter in a medium-sized non-stick skillet over medium low heat.
2. Whisk the eggs.
3. When the butter is just barely bubbling, add the eggs to the pan directly in the center so that the butter gets pushed out to the sides.
4. Watch for the edges to just barely start to set, and then gently swipe a spatula around the edges of the pan to create large soft curds. Don't flip the curds over.
5. Continue this process, pausing in between to allow time for the eggs to cook, but not to overcook. The entire process should take 2-3 minutes or less.
6. When the eggs are barely set and you have some big folds of heavenly soft scrambled eggs laying in the pan, remove from heat.
7. Serve on a breakfast sandwich.

Nutritional value (per serving)

- Calories: 168
- Fat: 12.5g
- Protein: 13g
- Carbs: 1g

CHOCOLATE CHIP, PB & BANANA SANDWICHES

Servings: 2

Prep time: 5 minutes

Total time: 10 minutes

Spoil your kids with this yummy grilled sandwich treat! Melted chocolate and peanut butter combined with slices of banana will have your children begging for this creamy and delicious snack or dessert.

Ingredients:

- 1/4 cup creamy peanut butter
- 2 tablespoons honey
- 1/4 teaspoon ground cinnamon
- 2 tablespoons miniature semisweet chocolate chips
- 4 slices whole wheat bread
- 1 medium banana, thinly sliced

Instructions

1. Mix peanut butter, honey, and cinnamon
2. Stir in chocolate chips. Spread over bread.
3. Layer two bread slices with banana slices
4. Top with remaining bread.
5. If desired, cut into shapes using cookie cutters.

Nutritional value (per serving)

- Calories: 502
- Fat: 22g
- Protein: 15g
- Carbs: 69g

BACON BREAKFAST PIZZA

Servings: 8

Prep time: 10 minutes

Total time: 30 minutes

Sometimes you may want something quick and light for breakfast, and other times you want something warm, savory, and filling. This breakfast pizza is perfect for satisfying those cravings.

Ingredients:

- 1 tube (13.8 ounces) refrigerated pizza crust
- 2 tablespoons olive oil, divided
- 6 large eggs
- 2 tablespoons water
- 1 package (3 ounces) bacon bits
- 1 cup shredded Monterey Jack cheese
- 1 cup shredded cheddar cheese

Instructions

1. Preheat oven to 400°.
2. Unroll and press dough onto bottom and 1/2-inch up sides of a greased 15x10x1-inch pan.
3. Prick dough thoroughly with a fork; brush with 1 tablespoon oil.
4. Bake until lightly browned, 7-8 minutes.
5. Meanwhile, whisk together eggs and water.
6. In a nonstick skillet, heat remaining oil over medium heat.
7. Add eggs; cook and stir just until thickened and no liquid egg remains.
8. Spoon over crust. Sprinkle with bacon bits and cheeses.
9. Bake until cheese is melted, 5-7 minutes.

Bacon breakfast pizza tips

1. Bacon should be cooked before putting it on pizza for two reasons: pizza has a short bake time so the bacon wouldn't cook through and the uncooked bacon would make the pizza greasy.

Nutritional value (per serving)

- Calories: 325
- Fat: 20g
- Protein: 20g
- Carbs: 24g

This Page Is Intentionally Left Blank

CHAPTER 7:
APPETIZER & SNACK RECIPES

MARSHMALLOW FRUIT DIP

Servings: 5 cups

Prep time: 10 minutes

Total time: 10 minutes

Two unlikely ingredients come together to make a divine treat – Fluffy Marshmallow Cream Cheese Fruit Dip. Serve with your favorite fresh fruits or cookies.

Ingredients:

- 1 package (8 ounces) cream cheese, softened
- ¾ cup cherry yogurt
- 1 carton (8 ounces) frozen whipped topping, thawed
- 1 jar (7 ounces) marshmallow creme
- Assorted fresh fruit

Instructions

1. In a large bowl, beat cream cheese and yogurt until blended.
2. Fold in whipped topping and marshmallow creme.
3. Serve with fruit.

Nutritional value (per serving)

- Calories: 56
- Fat: 3g
- Protein: 1g
- Carbs: 6g

LOADED BAKED POTATO DIP

Servings: 8

Prep time: 10 minutes

Total time: 10 minutes

I never thought of using waffle-cut fries as a scoop for dip until a friend of mine did at a baby shower. They're ideal for my cheesy bacon and chive dip, which tastes just like a baked potato topper.

Ingredients:

- 2 cups reduced-fat sour cream
- 2 cups shredded reduced-fat cheddar cheese
- 8 center-cut bacon or turkey bacon strips, chopped and cooked
- 1/3 cup minced fresh chives
- 2 teaspoons Louisiana-style hot sauce
- Hot cooked waffle-cut fries

Instructions

1. In a small bowl, mix the first 5 ingredients until blended
2. Refrigerate until serving.
3. Serve with waffle fries.

Nutritional value (per serving)

- Calories: 149
- Fat: 10g
- Protein: 11g
- Carbs: 4g

KIDDIE CRUNCH MIX

Servings: 6 cups

Prep time: 5 minutes

Total time: 10 minutes

This no-bake snack mix is a real treat for kids, and you can easily increase the amount to fit your needs. Place it in individual plastic bags or pour some into colored ice cream cones and cover with plastic wrap for a fun presentation.

Ingredients:

- 1 cup plain or frosted animal crackers
- 1 cup bear-shaped crackers
- 1 cup miniature pretzels
- 1 cup salted peanuts
- 1 cup M&M's
- 1 cup yogurt- or chocolate-covered raisins

Instructions

1. In a bowl, combine all ingredients.
2. Store in an airtight container.

Nutritional value (per serving)

- Calories: 266
- Fat: 14g
- Protein: 6g
- Carbs: 33g

PEANUT BUTTER GRANOLA PINWHEELS

Servings: 16

Prep time: 10 minutes

Total time: 10 minutes

Great for after school, it's really quick to make and filling enough to hold the kids until dinner. To satisfy heftier appetites or to serve as a power lunch, cut each tortilla into fewer pieces or provide one per child. The recipe is easy to increase as needed.

Ingredients:

- 4 tablespoons creamy peanut butter
- 2 flour tortillas (8 inches)
- 2 teaspoons honey
- 1/2 cup granola without raisins

Instructions

1. Spread peanut butter over each tortilla
2. Drizzle with honey and sprinkle with granola.
3. Roll up; cut into slices.

Nutritional value (per serving)

- Calories: 60
- Fat: 3g
- Protein: 2g
- Carbs: 7g

RANCH SNACK MIX

Servings: 32

Prep time: 5 minutes

Total time: 15 minutes

They are just so perfectly flavored, perfectly toasted and perfectly popable. They are sooo addicting!

Ingredients:

- 1 package (12 ounces) miniature pretzels
- 16 cups of Bugles (about 12 ounces)
- 1 can (10 ounces) salted cashews
- 1 package (6 ounces) Goldfish cheddar crackers
- 1 envelope of ranch salad dressing mix
- 3/4 cup canola oil

Instructions

1. In 2 large bowls, combine the pretzels, Bugles, cashews, and crackers.
2. Sprinkle with dressing mix; toss gently to combine.
3. Drizzle with oil; toss until well coated.
4. Store in airtight containers.

Nutritional value (per serving)

- Calories: 18
- Fat: 11g
- Protein: 4g
- Carbs: 19g

LEMON-APRICOT FRUIT POPS

Servings: 6

Prep time: 15 minutes

Total time: 15 minutes

With just 31 calories and less than 1 tsp. sugar per serving, this is one light and refreshing summer dessert everyone can find room for!

Ingredients:

- 1/4 cup orange juice
- 1 teaspoon grated lemon zest
- 1/4 cup lemon juice
- 4 teaspoons sugar
- 1 cup sliced fresh apricots (4-5 medium apricots)
- 1/2 cup ice cubes
- 1 teaspoon minced fresh mint, optional
- 6 freezer pop molds or 6 paper cups (3 ounces each) and wooden pop sticks

Instructions

1. Place the first 6 ingredients in a blender; cover and process until blended.
2. If desired, stir in mint.
3. Pour into molds or paper cups. Top molds with holders.
4. If using cups, top with foil and insert sticks through foil.
5. Freeze until firm.

Health tip:

1. There are only 11 little calories from the added sugar in these refreshing pops!

Nutritional value (per serving)

- Calories: 31
- Fat: 0g
- Protein: 0g
- Carbs: 8.5g

GLAZED DOUGHNUT HOLES

Servings: 1 dozen

Prep time: 5 minutes

Total time: 5 minutes

And a big congratulations to you, because you've just been appointed president of the No Sharing Club.

Ingredients:

- 2 cups confectioners' sugar
- 3 to 5 tablespoons frozen grape, cherry-pomegranate, or cranberry juice concentrate, thawed
- 12 doughnut holes

Lemon Variation:

- 2 cups confectioners' sugar
- 5 tablespoons lemon juice

Instructions

1. Whisk together sugar and enough juice concentrate to achieve a thick glaze.
2. Dip doughnut holes in glaze; transfer to waxed paper.
3. Variation: for lemon glaze, whisk together sugar and lemon juice until smooth.
4. Dip doughnut holes and transfer to waxed paper.

Nutritional value (per serving)

- Calories: 225
- Fat: 4g
- Protein: 1g
- Carbs: 49g

GRANOLA TRAIL MIX

Servings: 11

Prep time: 5 minutes

Total time: 5 minutes

Three loves of mine: fluffy blankets, granola, and trail mix. Let's combine two out of three... actually, if I count all the trail mix granola crumbs spilled on my fluffy blanket while watching TV/munching then we have a tasty (and messy) triple threat.

Ingredients:

- 1 package (16 oz) banana-nut granola
- 1 package (15 oz) raisins
- 1 package (12.6 oz) milk chocolate M&M's
- 1 can (12 oz) honey-roasted peanuts

Instructions

1. Place all ingredients in a large bowl; toss to combine.
2. Store in airtight containers.

Nutritional value (per serving)

- Calories: 331
- Fat: 15g
- Protein: 7g
- Carbs: 46g

CHEDDAR CORN DOG MUFFINS

Servings: 9

Prep time: 15 minutes

Total time: 25 minutes

Hormones are NO joke, people. NO JOKE. Some of my favorite memories involve being in the kitchen with my mama and I really couldn't wait to get into the kitchen with my kids!

Ingredients:

- 1 package (8½ ounces) cornbread/muffin mix
- 2/3 cup of 2% milk
- 1 large room-temperature egg, lightly beaten,
- 5 turkey hot dogs, sliced
- 1/2 cup shredded sharp cheddar cheese
- 2 tablespoons finely chopped pickled jalapenos, optional

Instructions

1. Preheat oven to 400°. Line 9 muffin cups with foil liners or grease 9 nonstick muffin cups.
2. In a small bowl, combine muffin mix, milk, and egg
3. Stir in hot dogs, cheese, and, if desired, jalapenos.
4. Fill prepared cups three-quarters full.
5. Bake until a toothpick inserted in center comes out clean, 14-18 minutes.
6. Cool 5 minutes before removing from pan to a wire rack.
7. Serve warm & Refrigerate leftovers.

Freezing option:

1. Freeze cooled muffins in freezer containers.
2. To use, microwave each muffin on high until heated through, 30-60 seconds.

Nutritional value (per serving)

- Calories: 216
- Fat: 10g
- Protein: 8g
- Carbs: 23g

TEXAS TUMBLEWEEDS

Servings: 4 dozen

Prep time: 10 minutes

Total time: 20 minutes

If you love salty sweet treats you better watch out for these bad boys. The combination of flavors is amazing. I just kind of want to coat everything with the peanut butter butterscotch mixture.

Ingredients:

- 1 cup butterscotch chips
- 1 cup creamy peanut butter
- 1 can (9 ounces) potato sticks (about 6 cups)

Instructions

1. In a large microwave-safe bowl in a microwave or in a large metal bowl over simmering water, melt butterscotch chips and peanut butter
2. Stir until smooth. Gently stir in potato sticks.
3. Drop rounded tablespoonfuls of the mixture onto baking paper-lined baking sheets.
4. Refrigerate 10-15 minutes or until set.

Test Kitchen tips

1. Swap chocolate chips for the butterscotch and Nutella for the peanut butter. Heavenly!
2. No potato sticks on hand? Try using crushed potato chips.

Nutritional value (per serving)

- Calories: 76
- Fat: 5g
- Protein: 2g
- Carbs: 6g

This Page Is Intentionally Left Blank

CHAPTER 8:
LUNCH RECIPES

TURKEY RANCH WRAPS

Servings: 4

Prep time: 10 minutes

Total time: 10 minutes

Don't forget to throw in some fruits and veggies to help your kids have a well rounded meal! (And make sure to pack lunch with ice to keep meat and other ingredients fresh and cold).

Ingredients:

- 8 thin slices of cooked turkey
- 4 flour tortillas (6 inches), room temperature
- 1 large tomato, thinly sliced
- 1 medium green pepper, cut into thin strips
- 1 cup shredded lettuce
- 1 cup shredded cheddar cheese
- 1/3 cup ranch salad dressing

Instructions

1. Place 2 slices of turkey on each tortilla.
2. Layer with tomato, green pepper, lettuce, and cheese.
3. Drizzle with salad dressing.
4. Roll up tightly.

Nutritional value (per serving)

- Calories: 403
- Fat: 25g
- Protein: 26g
- Carbs: 19g

CHICKEN & BACON ROLL-UPS

Servings: 4 dozen

Prep time: 15 minutes

Total time: 1 hour 15 minutes

Minimal ingredients, super delicious, and budget friendly.

Ingredients:

- 1 can (9 ounces) chunky white chicken, drained
- 1 carton (8 ounces) spreadable garden vegetable cream cheese
- 1 cup salsa, divided
- 4 pieces ready-to-serve fully cooked bacon, crumbled
- 6 flour tortillas (8 inches), room temperature

Instructions

1. Mix chicken, cream cheese, 1/2 cup salsa, and bacon.
2. Spread over tortillas.
3. Roll up tightly and wrap in plastic.
4. Refrigerate for at least 1 hour.
5. Just before serving, unwrap and cut tortillas into 1-inch slices.
6. Serve with remaining salsa.

Nutritional value (per serving)

- Calories: 43
- Fat: 2g
- Protein: 3g
- Carbs: 4g

CHEESY QUESADILLAS

Servings: 6

Prep time: 10 minutes

Total time: 15 minutes

My only other word of advice is to keep it simple with the fillings. Stick to just a few ingredients and only use about 1/2 cup or so per quesadilla. The melted cheese will hold the filling in place once the tortilla is folded and help prevent it from tumbling out on the plate.

Ingredients:

- 4 flour tortillas (8 inches), warmed
- 1½ cups shredded Mexican cheese blend
- 1/2 cup salsa

Instructions

1. Place the tortillas on a greased baking sheet.
2. Combine the cheese and salsa; spread over half of each tortilla. Fold over.
3. Broil 4 inches from the heat for 3 minutes on each side or until golden brown.
4. Cut into wedges.

Nutritional value (per serving)

- Calories: 223
- Fat: 11g
- Protein: 9g
- Carbs: 21g

BLT WRAPS

Servings: 8

Prep time: 10 minutes

Total time: 15 minutes

My mom and I used to make these easy wrap-ups for summer days at the lake with our entire family. These days, we love to bring them to picnics and days in the park.

Ingredients:

- 16 ready-to-serve fully cooked bacon strips, warmed if desired
- 8 flour tortillas (8 inches), room temperature
- 4 cups chopped lettuce
- 2 cups chopped tomatoes (3 small tomatoes)
- 2 cups shredded cheddar cheese
- 1/2 cup ranch salad dressing

Instructions

1. Place 2 bacon strips across the center of each tortilla.
2. Top with lettuce, tomatoes, and cheese; drizzle with salad dressing.
3. Fold 1 side of the tortilla over the filling and roll up.

To make ahead:

1. Assemble wraps without heating bacon.
2. Wrap in plastic wrap and store in refrigerator for up to 2 days.

Nutritional value (per serving)

- Calories: 409
- Fat: 25g
- Protein: 15g
- Carbs: 31g

BBQ CHICKEN

Servings: 4

Prep time: 7 minutes

Total time: 12 minutes

The onions work double duty for this recipe. After roasting, they're not only super delicious, they also add extra moisture to the pan and will keep the sauce from burning.

Ingredients

- 4 chicken breasts
- 1/2 cup barbecue sauce
- 1/4 cup cheddar cheese
- 2-3 tablespoons bacon bits, optional

Instructions

1. Place chicken breasts in a microwave dish. Top with sauce.
2. Cook in the microwave for 4-5 minutes.
3. Sprinkle with cheddar cheese and bacon bits.
4. Cook in the microwave for another 3-4 minutes.

Nutritional value (per serving)

- Calories: 210
- Fat: 12g
- Protein: 25g
- Carbs: 0g

MANGO MONDAY MEAT LOAF

Servings: 2

Prep time: 5 minutes

Total time: 25 minutes

This delicious and tender meatloaf with a super easy mango glaze is the best meatloaf recipe you'll ever try! The sweet and sour flavors of the glaze really compliment the savory meatloaf, this is sure to become a favorite at your house.

Ingredients

- 1 lb lean ground beef
- 1 cup chopped mango
- 1 cup breadcrumbs
- 1 egg
- 1 onion, grated
- salt and pepper to taste

Instructions

1. Combine all ingredients in a bowl and mix together with your hands.
2. Form into a loaf and place in a glass loaf pan.
3. Cover with microwave-safe baking paper
4. Cook in the microwave for 15-20 minutes.

Nutritional value (per serving)

- Calories: 733
- Fat: 41g
- Protein: 39g
- Carbs: 49g

CHEESE FRIES

Servings: 8

Prep time: 5 minutes

Total time: 20 minutes

Ingredients:

- 1 package (28 ounces) frozen steak fries
- 1 can (10¾ ounces) condensed cheddar cheese soup, undiluted
- 1/4 cup 2% milk
- 1/2 teaspoon garlic powder
- 1/4 teaspoon onion powder
- Paprika

Instructions

2. Arrange the steak fries in a single layer in 2 greased 15x10x1-inch baking pans.
3. Bake at 450° for 15-18 minutes or until tender and golden brown.
4. Meanwhile, in a saucepan, combine soup, milk, garlic powder, and onion powder; heat through.
5. Drizzle the mixture over the fries; sprinkle with paprika.

Nutritional value (per serving)

- Calories: 129
- Fat: 5g
- Protein: 3g
- Carbs: 20g

LUNCH BOX PIZZAS

Servings: 10

Prep time: 5 minutes

Total time: 20 minutes

When you have these fun-to-make mini pizzas, it's no challenge finding lunch fare that the kids enjoy. Plus they pack nicely in sandwich bags and travel well, so there's no mess.

Ingredients:

- 1 tube (7-1/2 ounces) refrigerated buttermilk biscuits (10 biscuits)
- 1/4 cup tomato sauce
- 1 teaspoon Italian seasoning
- 10 slices of pepperoni
- 3/4 cup shredded Monterey Jack cheese

Instructions

1. Flatten each biscuit into a 3-in. circle and press into a greased muffin cup.
2. Combine the tomato sauce and Italian seasoning; spoon 1 teaspoonful of sauce into each cup.
3. Top each with a slice of pepperoni and about 1 tablespoon of cheese.
4. Bake at 425° until golden brown, 10-15 minutes.
5. Serve immediately or store in the refrigerator.

Nutritional value (per serving)

- Calories: 94
- Fat: 4g
- Protein: 4g
- Carbs: 11g

CREAMY CHICKEN ALFREDO

Servings: 4

Prep time: 25 minutes

Total time: 60 minutes

This Chicken Fettuccine Alfredo is a super simple yet delicious recipe to make for a restaurant quality dish, ready in just 40 minutes. So creamy and cheesy!

Ingredients:

- 2 boneless, skinless chicken breasts, diced
- 1 8-oz. package of fettuccine noodles, cooked and drained
- 2 cups whipping cream
- 6 cloves of garlic, peeled and crushed
- 2 cups shredded Parmesan cheese
- 2 tablespoons butter
- 1/2 teaspoon salt
- 1/4 teaspoon nutmeg
- 1 tablespoon oregano

Instructions

1. Cook fettuccine noodles according to package directions and set aside.
2. In a large saucepan, saute diced chicken in 2 tablespoons of oil.
3. Cook until no longer pink and juices run clear. Add garlic and cook for one minute.
4. Add seasonings, butter, whipping cream, and cheese.
5. Cook on medium-low heat until cheese is melted and all ingredients are thoroughly incorporated throughout the dish.
6. Serve Alfredo sauce over prepared noodles.

Nutritional value (per serving)

- Calories: 400
- Fat: 22g
- Protein: 14g
- Carbs: 36g

RAINBOW SPAGHETTI

Servings: 4

Prep time: 15 minutes

Total time: 32 minutes

Try making this rainbow spaghetti as a sensory activity for babies and toddlers, or serve as a fun lunch – just top with their favourite dressing, and enjoy with a salad.

Ingredients:

- 200g spaghetti
- a mix of food colorings

To serve (optional)

- salad dressing or melted butter
- 50g cheddar, grated
- mixed salad leaves and veg

Instructions

1. Cook the spaghetti following the package instructions.
2. Drain, then divide between bowls based on the number of colours you'd like to use.
3. Add a drop of food coloring to each bowl or combine two colors.
4. Mix well, adding a splash of water to help the color disperse, if needed.
5. Leave for 5 mins, then rinse the spaghetti under cold running water to set the color.
6. Toss with some salad dressing or melted butter.
7. Top with a little grated cheese and a salad of mixed leaves and vegetables.

Nutritional value (per serving)

- Calories: 268
- Fat: 8g
- Protein: 10g
- Carbs: 38g

SWEET AND SOUR CHICKEN

Servings: 4

Prep time: 15 minutes

Total time: 40 minutes

This recipe calls for chicken breasts, but you could use thighs as well. You want boneless, skinless thighs though.

Ingredients

- 1 tablespoon butter
- 4 chicken breasts or pork loin, cut in cubes
- 1 can pineapple chunks (save juice)
- 1 garlic clove
- 2-3 tablespoons soy sauce
- 1 teaspoon ginger
- 1 teaspoon cornstarch

Instructions

1. Cook chicken or pork in butter, add garlic and sauté.
2. Drain pineapple juice into pan.
3. Add soy sauce, ginger, and cornstarch – just enough to thicken.
4. Let simmer for several minutes, then add pineapple chunks and serve over rice.

Nutritional value (per serving)

- Calories: 310
- Fat: 14g
- Protein: 18g
- Carbs: 28g

INDONESIAN CHICKEN SATAY

Servings: 2

Prep time: 15 minutes

Total time: 45 minutes

Many South East Asian countries have a version of Satay Chicken. This Indonesian version is the easiest, you can get everything you need from the supermarket and it is SO tasty. This peanut sauce is thick and chunky, not a thin dipping sauce.

Ingredients

- bamboo skewers
- 1 cup unsweetened coconut milk
- 1 ½ teaspoon curry powder
- 1/2 teaspoon ground coriander
- 1 tablespoon soy sauce
- 1-2 cloves of garlic, finely chopped
- 2 teaspoons cornstarch
- 1 lb. chicken breasts, cut into strips

Instruction

1. Soak bamboo skewers in water for about 30 minutes.
2. In a medium bowl, add coconut milk, curry powder, coriander, soy sauce, garlic, and cornstarch.
3. Blend together.
4. Add strips of chicken breasts. Marinate for several hours or overnight.
5. Thread each chicken strip onto a bamboo skewer and grill.
6. Serve with a peanut sauce.

Nutritional value (per serving)

- Calories: 449
- Fat: 27g
- Protein: 37.8g
- Carbs: 15g

SPAGHETTI CUPCAKES

Servings: 2

Prep time: 15 minutes

Total time: 35 minutes

These Spaghetti "Cupcakes" look like little bird nests. They are not only super simple to make but they are kid-friendly and an easy, fun meal to make with kids! They are handheld spaghetti cups! Who wouldn't love that?!

Ingredients

- 8 ounces cooked spaghetti
- 4 eggs
- 1/2 cup Parmesan cheese
- 1 jar of spaghetti sauce
- 2 cups mozzarella cheese

Instructions

1. Have an adult cook the spaghetti and set it aside.
2. In a bowl, beat eggs, then add Parmesan cheese, and spaghetti noodles. Stir to combine.
3. Grease muffin tins and press noodles into muffin cups.
4. Top each with sauce and mozzarella cheese.
5. Have an adult bake them for 15 minutes at 375 degrees.

Nutritional value (per serving)

- Calories: 460
- Fat: 25g
- Protein: 24g
- Carbs: 32g

This Page Is Intentionally Left Blank

CHAPTER 9:
DINNER RECIPES

CHICKEN AND PEA CASSEROLE

Servings: 4

Prep time: 20 minutes

Total time: 55 minutes

This simple dish of beautifully seasoned chicken and peas is the meal solution you're looking for when you're short on time but want something tasty and healthy!

Ingredients

- 4 chicken breasts (or one for each person)
- 1 can of cream mushroom soup
- 1 cup milk
- 1/2 bag of frozen peas and carrots
- 1 cup cheddar cheese, shredded
- Pepper, and paprika to taste
- breadcrumbs for topping

Instructions

1. In a casserole dish, place the chicken breasts on the bottom of the pan. Add peas on top of chicken.
2. In a medium bowl, add mushroom soup and milk. Stir until well blended.
3. Season with pepper and paprika but no salt. The mushroom soup will have salt in it already.
4. Spread mushroom soup over the top of the chicken breasts.
5. Bake for 35-40 minutes at 375 degrees.
6. Top with cheddar cheese and bake until cheese is melted.

Nutritional value (per serving)

- Calories: 129
- Fat: 4.7g
- Protein: 7.4g
- Carbs: 14.5g

HAM, MACARONI, AND CHEESE CHOWDER

Servings: 4

Prep time: 10 minutes

Total time: 30 minutes

The kids will especially love this Macaroni & Cheese Chowder. By adding ham and corn, this cheesy creamy dish gets an instant upgrade.

Ingredients

- 1 (14 oz.) can of chicken broth
- 1 cup of water
- 1 cup of elbow macaroni or other shape
- 1 cup frozen corn
- 1 cup frozen peas and carrots
- 1 cup cooked ham, diced
- 6 oz. of American cheese, cubed
- 1 cup milk

Instructions

1. Pour the chicken broth and water into a large saucepan.
2. Place the pan over high heat and bring to a brisk boil.
3. Pour in the macaroni. Reduce the heat to medium low.
4. Simmer for 12 minutes or until the macaroni is tender. Do not drain.
5. Stir in the corn, peas and carrots, ham, and cheese cubes.
6. Pour the milk into the pan and stir until blended in well.
7. Cook, stirring often, for 5 minutes or until the cheese has completely melted.

Nutritional value (per serving)

- Calories: 142
- Fat: 4.6g
- Protein: 13g
- Carbs: 12g

POTATO CHICKEN CASSEROLE

Servings: 3

Prep time: 15 minutes

Total time: 45 minutes

Loaded Potato Ranch Chicken Casserole is a whole dinner in one! All topped with melty cheese and bacon. It is heaven on a plate!

Ingredients

- 2-3 potatoes, shredded
- 6-8 chicken breasts, cubed
- 1 tablespoon oil
- seasoning salt
- 1 tablespoon butter
- 2 tablespoons flour
- 1 1/2 cup milk
- 1/4 cup shredded cheese
- 1/4 cup Parmesan cheese
- salt and pepper
- 1/4 teaspoon basil

Instructions

1. In a saucepan, melt butter and whisk in flour, making a roux.
2. Whisk in milk and simmer until it thickens. Add cheese and seasonings.
3. Continue to simmer until cheese melts.
4. Mix chicken breasts, cooked peas and carrots
5. Layer chicken and vegetables on top of the potatoes.
6. Spread sauce over the top, stir to combine.
7. Bake for 20 minutes at 350 degrees.

Nutritional value (per serving)

- Calories: 354
- Fat: 15g
- Protein: 23g
- Carbs: 31g

HAM BEAN SOUP

Servings: 4

Prep time: 12 minutes

Total time: 30 minutes

If you like ham and bean soup but don't want to spend hours in the kitchen, this tasty, quick version will leave you with a satisfied smile.

Ingredients

- 3 cups white beans, canned
- 1 onion, quartered
- 2 bay leaves
- 1-2 potatoes, cubed
- 2 carrots, cubed
- 1 cup chopped ham
- salt and pepper
- 2 tablespoons Italian seasoning
- 1 teaspoon cajun seasoning

Instructions

1. In a pot, add potatoes, carrots, and beans.
2. Add more water if needed to cover all the vegetables.
3. Add in spices. Bring to a boil and cook until potatoes are tender.
4. Taste test and add more seasoning as needed.

Nutritional value (per serving)

- Calories: 177
- Fat: 2g
- Protein: 14g
- Carbs: 22g

SKILLET PIZZA

Servings: 4

Prep time: 15 minutes

Total time: 45 minutes

Revolutionize your homemade pizza with this cast iron skillet pizza. The most crispy, crunchy crust that is developed through high heat and is the best homemade pizza I've ever made.

Ingredients

- Flour or Multigrain tortilla (smaller than burrito size)
- 1/4 cup of tomato sauce or pizza sauce
- 1/4 tsp each of dried oregano and dried basil
- 1 tsp grated Parmesan
- 1/2 cup shredded low-fat mozzarella
- ¼ cup toppings of choice (optional) (e.g. veg, turkey pepperoni, etc.)
- Non-stick cooking spray, olive oil flavor

Instructions

1. Spray non-stick pan with cooking spray.
2. Place the naked tortilla in the cold pan.
3. Spread sauce on top of tortilla and sprinkle with dried seasonings and Parmesan cheese.
4. Spread the mozzarella and add toppings on top of cheese.
5. Turn the heat on for the skillet to medium and allow the tortilla to toast to the desired color.
6. Carefully slide the "pizza" onto a plate and let it sit for 1 minute to cool slightly and get crunchy.
7. Slice into quarters and serve with a small salad.

Nutritional value (per serving)

- Calories: 310
- Fat: 51g
- Protein: 37g
- Carbs: 2.5g

PIZZA SOUP

Servings: 6

Prep time: 10 minutes

Total time: 30 minutes

This robust soup is a family favorite, and it's a big hit with my canasta group as well. I top each bowl with a slice of toasted bread and cheese, but you can have fun incorporating other pizza toppings such as cooked sausage.

Ingredients

- 8 oz. (2 small cans) sliced mushrooms
- 1 can black olives sliced
- 4 cups water
- 15 oz. of pizza sauce or spaghetti sauce
- 2 tablespoons Italian seasoning
- Chopped pepperoni
- Chopped Canadian bacon
- Chopped green peppers or other favorite pizza toppings

Instructions

1. Mix all ingredients together and simmer for 15-20 minutes.
2. Serve with breadsticks or French bread.

Nutritional value (per serving)

- Calories: 280
- Fat: 14g
- Protein: 14g
- Carbs: 27g

CHILI MAC SUPPER

Servings: 4

Prep time: 15 minutes

Total time: 35 minutes

Whether you're at a tailgate party or tucked warm and cozy inside watching your favorite team on the TV with your favorite people, this hearty Chili Mac Recipe will please a crowd.

Ingredients

- 1 cup of uncooked macaroni
- 1 lb. lean ground beef
- 1/2 tsp chili powder
- 1 (11.25 oz.) can chili beef soup
- 1 (14.5 oz.) can diced tomatoes
- 1/2 cup of cheddar cheese, shredded

Instructions

1. Cook pasta according to directions.
2. Meanwhile place ground beef in a bowl and stir in chili powder.
3. Drain pasta and add into soup pot.
4. Stir in tomatoes, chili beef soup, and cooked macaroni.
5. Warm and serve each bowl of chili mac with cheddar cheese.

Nutritional value (per serving)

- Calories: 211
- Fat: 2g
- Protein: 12g
- Carbs: 38g

CREAMY BEEF NOODLES

Servings: 4

Prep time: 10 minutes

Total time: 30 minutes

Ingredients

- 1 pound of ground hamburger
- 1 can of cream of mushroom soup
- 1 (4-ounce) can of mushroom pieces
- 4 cups of uncooked noodles
- 1 ½ tablespoons of mustard
- 2 ½ cups of water
- 1 tablespoon of parsley, flaked
- 2-quart glass casserole dish

Instructions

1. Place beef inside casserole pan, breaking it up with a fork and distributing evenly along the bottom.
2. Put casserole dish in the microwave for 6-8 minutes to cook the meat.
3. Drain as much fat out of the casserole pan as possible.
4. Stir the meat around again with a whisk or another large utensil to crumble further.
5. Add remaining ingredients to the casserole pan, mixing them with the hamburger meat until distributed evenly throughout the mixture.
6. Cover your dish and microwave the concoction for 15-17 minutes until the noodles are tender, remembering to stir occasionally throughout the process.
7. Let cool to a tolerable level before serving.

Nutritional value (per serving)

- Calories: 334
- Fat: 9.3g
- Protein: 25.6g
- Carbs: 37g

GARLIC BREAD PIZZA SANDWICHES

Servings: 4

Prep time: 10 minutes

Total time: 20 minutes

Feel free to customize with any of your favorite pizza toppings!

Ingredients:

- 1 package (11 ¼ ounces) frozen garlic Texas toast
- 1/4 cup pasta sauce
- 4 slices of provolone cheese
- 16 slices of pepperoni
- 8 slices thinly cut hard salami
- Additional pasta sauce, warmed, optional

Instructions

1. Preheat griddle over medium-low heat.
2. Add garlic toast; cook until lightly browned, 3-4 minutes per side.
3. Spoon 1 tablespoon of sauce over each of the 4 pieces of toast.
4. Top with cheese, pepperoni, salami, and remaining toast.
5. Cook until crisp and cheese is melted, 3-5 minutes, turning as necessary.
6. If desired, serve with additional sauce.

Nutritional value (per serving)

- Calories: 456
- Fat: 28g
- Protein: 19g
- Carbs: 36g

FRUITY CHICKEN SALAD PITAS

Servings: 2

Prep time: 5 minutes

Total time: 15 minutes

I found this handwritten recipe tucked inside an old community cookbook I bought more than 40 years ago. I made a few changes over the years to suit my family's tastes.

Ingredients:

- 1 cup cubed rotisserie chicken
- 1/2 cup chopped apple
- 1/2 cup chopped celery
- 1/2 cup unsweetened crushed pineapple, well drained
- 1/4 cup dried cranberries
- 1/4 cup mayonnaise
- 1 teaspoon lemon juice
- 1/4 teaspoon onion powder
- 1/8 teaspoon salt
- 4 pita pocket halves

Instructions

1. Combine the first 9 ingredients.
2. Fill pita halves with chicken mixture.

Nutritional value (per serving)

- Calories: 588
- Fat: 26g
- Protein: 26g
- Carbs: 63g

GARLIC TOAST PIZZAS

Servings: 8

Prep time: 5 minutes

Total time: 15 minutes

Between working full-time, going to school and raising three children, finding time-saving recipes that my family likes is one of my biggest challenges. These quick pizzas pack a huge amount of flavor.

Ingredients:

- 1 package (11¼ ounces) frozen garlic Texas toast.
- 1/2 cup pizza sauce.
- 1 package (3½ ounces) sliced regular or turkey pepperoni.
- 2 cups shredded part-skim mozzarella cheese.

Instructions

1. Preheat oven to 425°. Place Texas toast in a 15x10x1-in. baking pan.
2. Bake for 5 minutes.
3. Spread toast with pizza sauce; top with pepperoni and cheese.
4. Bake until cheese is melted, 4-5 minutes longer.

Nutritional value (per serving)

- Calories: 281
- Fat: 20g
- Protein: 12g
- Carbs: 14g

CREAMY TUNA SKILLET

Servings: 6

Prep time: 10 minutes

Total time: 25 minutes

Your favorite comfort food — tuna casserole: reinvented! This creamy tuna pasta with peas is made in one skillet.

Ingredients:

- 4 oz. of angel hair pasta that has been cooked and drained in a skillet with olive oil and water
- 5 oz. Prime Fillet Albacore tuna with sun-ripened tomatoes and olive oil
- 1 garlic clove, minced
- 1/2 cup additional sun-ripened tomatoes
- 1/2 cup freshly chopped basil
- 1 15-oz. can of condensed cream of mushroom soup
- 3/4 cup grated Parmesan cheese
- 1 1/2 cups of water
- 1/4 teaspoon salt

Instructions

1. In the same skillet that you cooked the angel hair pasta in, heat 2 tablespoons of olive oil on medium-high heat.
2. Once heated, cook garlic clove until soft. Add remaining ingredients and stir well.
3. Cook on medium-high heat until mixture comes to a boil.
4. Reduce heat and simmer for 10 minutes, stirring intermittently.
5. Garnish with additional unripened tomatoes, fresh basil, and Parmesan cheese.
6. Enjoy!

Nutritional value (per serving)

- Calories: 375
- Fat: 7g
- Protein: 22g
- Carbs: 55.6g

BACON GRILLED CHEESE

Servings: 2

Prep time: 10 minutes

Total time: 25 minutes

What kind of magic is this?! Combining bacon with cheddar and pepper jack cheeses takes a classic grilled cheese sandwich to the next level!

Perfect for lunch served alongside tomato soup or great for game day or movie night. Grilled cheese with bacon is a fancy, filling and flavorful take on a family favorite!

Ingredients:

- 4 slices of sourdough bread
- 2 tablespoons mayonnaise
- 6 slices of bacon
- 2 ounces cheddar cheese
- 2 ounces pepper jack cheese

Instructions

1. Cook bacon in a pan until crisp.
2. Remove from pan and drain, reserving 1 tablespoon of drippings in the pan.
3. Spread mayonnaise over the outside of each slice of bread.
4. Divide the cheese and bacon over 2 slices of bread and top with remaining bread.
5. Preheat a small skillet over low heat.
6. Grill sandwich until golden, about 4-5 minutes.
7. Flip and grill the other side until golden.

Nutritional value (per serving)

- Calories: 960
- Fat: 57g
- Protein: 38g
- Carbs: 74g

EASY KETO CHEESY BACON

Servings: 4

Prep time: 5 minutes

Total time: 40 minutes

It can be on the crumbly side if you try to cut it straight away, so if you can resist, let it cool down first. Out of the fridge is always best.

Ingredients:

- 4 large eggs
- 2 cups crumbled bacon cooked and drained
- 3 plum tomatoes diced
- 1 large onion diced
- 2 tablespoons butter
- 1 1/2 cups heavy whipping cream
- 1 cup shredded cheddar cheese
- 1/4 cup grated Parmesan cheese
- 1/4 teaspoon salt
- 1/8 teaspoon black pepper

Instructions

1. Preheat oven to 350 degrees Fahrenheit.
2. Mix eggs, whipping cream, salt, and pepper together in one bowl and set aside.
3. In a large skillet, heat 2 tablespoons of butter and saute the onion and plum tomatoes until tender.
4. Place onions, tomatoes, bacon, and half of the Parmesan and cheddar cheese in a bowl. Stir thoroughly.
5. Pour this mixture into a greased pie or quiche baking pan.
6. Gently pour egg and cream mixture on top.
7. Top with remaining cheese and bake for 35 minutes or until quiche is set.

Nutritional value (per serving)

- Calories: 761
- Fat: 68g
- Protein: 32g
- Carbs: 3.6g

CHICKEN PHILLY CHEESESTEAK

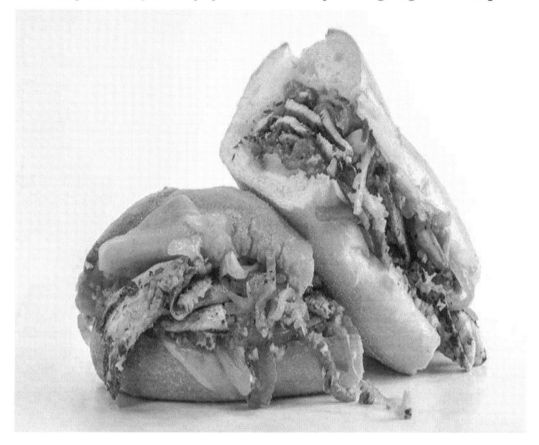

Servings: 6

Prep time: 15 minutes

Total time: 40 minutes

Don't get us wrong, we love the steak in a classic philly cheesesteak. But we heart chicken even more. So we created a semi-lighter version by sautéing thinly sliced chicken breast alongside onions and peppers. Don't worry, the whole thing still gets covered with cheese—provolone, not Cheez Whiz!

Ingredients:

- 1 red bell pepper, cut into thin strips
- 1 green pepper, cut into thin strips
- 1 large onion, cut into thin strips
- 6 boneless, skinless chicken breats, cut into thin strips
- 2 cups shredded mozzerella cheese
- Hoagie Buns or Baguette
- Olive Oil

Instructions

1. Saute half of the onions and half of the chicken in four tablespoons of olive oil in one large skillet.
2. Once peppers and onions are tender and chicken is cooked through, remove from heat.
3. Add one cup of mozzerella cheese. Stir until melted.
4. Repeat process for remaining peppers, onions, and chicken.
5. Once all the chicken and peppers are cooked, place on mayonnaise-covered bread and enjoy!

Nutritional value (per serving)

- Calories: 647
- Fat: 27g
- Protein: 45g
- Carbs: 55g

HOMEMADE HAM, TURKEY, AND CHEESE POCKETS

Servings: 8

Prep time: 15 minutes

Total time: 45 minutes

Ingredients:

- 1 (17-oz) box of puff pastry sheets
- 2 (2-oz) or larger packages of thinly sliced ham, Buddig brand
- 2 (2-oz) or larger packages of thinly sliced turkey
- 4 slices mild cheddar cheese
- 4 slices provolone cheese
- 2 onions diced and sautéed in two tablespoons of butter
- 1 green pepper diced and sautéed in two tablespoons of butter
- 1 large egg, whisked

Instructions

1. Cut each pastry sheet into quarters and roll each square slightly thinner.
2. Add 2 slices of ham, 2 slices of turkey, 1/2 slice of cheddar, 1/2 slice of provolone cheese, a teaspoon of onion, and a teaspoon of the green pepper to half of each square.
3. Brush whisked egg on the edges of the half of the square with meat and cheese, so you can fold over the top and seal the edges.
4. Fold over the top half of the dough and pinch the edges or crimp them with a fork to seal the dough together.
5. Place pockets on a parchment or lined baking sheet.
6. Cut a few slits on top of each pocket with a knife for ventilation, and then brush the tops with the whisked egg. Bake at 400 degrees Fahrenheit for 15 to 25 minutes.

Nutritional value (per serving)

- Calories: 505
- Fat: 27g
- Protein: 31g
- Carbs: 34g

SOUTHERN SALMON STEW

Servings: 3

Prep time: 5 minutes

Total time: 15 minutes

Taste a classic southern family friendly dish in a whole new way! Our Southern Salmon Stew uses Wild Pink Salmon, red potatoes, diced only, heavy cream and rice. To reduce the fat content, substitute whole milk or 2% milk for the heavy cream. The stew won't be quite as thick, but it will still be yummy!

Ingredients:

- 1 quart of milk (whole or evaporated)
- 1 ½ (5-oz.) cans of salmon (boneless, skinless)
- 2 tablespoons butter
- 4 tablespoons bacon (crumbled, optional)
- 1 tablespoon Italian seasoning
- 1 cup cooked potatoes (diced, optional)
- 1 cup of croutons (optional)
- 1/4 teaspoon ground peppercorn or black pepper
- salt to taste

Instructions

1. Heat salmon, milk, and butter on medium-low heat for three minutes and stir.
2. Add seasonings and optional potatoes, if desired.
3. Cook additional 7 minutes and serve.
4. Top with crumbled bacon and croutons, if desired.

Nutritional value (per serving)

- Calories: 269
- Fat: 21g
- Protein: 10g
- Carbs: 10g

CHICKEN MEATBALL SOUP

Servings: 10

Prep time: 5 minutes

Total time: 10 minutes

You'll only want this version of chicken noodle soup after trying this! Promise!

Ingredients

- 6 oz. ground turkey or chicken
- large beaten egg
- 3 tablespoons breadcrumbs
- parsley
- 1 teaspoon salt
- ¼ teaspoon pepper
- 6 cups chicken broth
- 2 medium carrots, peeled and sliced
- 1 cup potatoes, chopped

Instructions

1. Combine turkey, egg, bread crumbs, and parsley and form into meatballs.
2. In a saucepan, cook broth and add carrots.
3. Bring to a boil and add pasta, cook for 5 minutes.
4. Lower heat and add meatballs.
5. Simmer until cooked through.

Nutritional value (per serving)

- Calories: 190
- Fat: 2.8g
- Protein: 28g
- Carbs: 11g

EASY HOMEMADE CHICKEN NOODLE SOUP

Servings: 4

Prep time: 20 minutes

Total time: 1 hour 20 minutes

Ingredients

- Roast chicken or chicken pieces
- 1-2 carrots, cut in half
- 1 onion
- celery ribs with leaves
- 2 bay leaves

Instructions

1. Peel and cut the ends off of the carrots. Cut the carrots into 3 pieces. Cut celery ribs in half. Cut onion into quarters.
2. In a soup pot, add the roast chicken, carrots, a quartered onion, 1-2 celery leaves, and bay leaves.
3. Cover with water and bring to a boil. Cook and simmer on medium-low heat for 1 hour.
4. Drain broth and reserve. Allow chicken to cool slightly and shred.
5. Add another carrot, diced, and whatever vegetables you'd like to the broth.
6. Stir in egg noodles and simmer until vegetables and noodles are tender.

Nutritional value (per serving)

- Calories: 351
- Fat: 4.5g
- Protein: 40g
- Carbs: 37g

CHICKEN RICE SOUP

Servings: 4

Prep time: 5 minutes

Total time: 30 minutes

This easy Chicken Rice Soup recipe is a healthy soup that's perfect for chilly days! It's loaded with vegetables and brown rice, simmered in chicken broth and finished with a touch of creaminess.

Ingredients

- 6-8 cups chicken broth
- 2 cups brown rice
- 2 carrots, diced
- 2 celery ribs, diced

Instructions

1. Add whatever other vegetables you choose or have on hand.
2. Add all ingredients into a soup pot.
3. Let simmer until rice is tender and vegetables are done.
4. Cook brown rice before adding to broth.

Nutritional value (per serving)

- Calories: 253
- Fat: 4g
- Protein: 16g
- Carbs: 38g

TRADITIONAL TUNA SALAD

Servings: 4

Prep time: 10 minutes

Total time: 10 minutes

I like to make a big batch of this on Friday, so we have quick lunches/dinners all weekend.

Ingredients

- 1-2 cans of tuna, drained
- 2-3 tablespoons mayonnaise, as much as desired
- Chopped pickles

Instructions

1. Stir all ingredients together and serve on bread or crackers.

Nutritional value (per serving)

- Calories: 157
- Fat: 7.7g
- Protein: 12.7g
- Carbs: 12g

EASY KOREAN BBQ MARINADE

Servings: 6

Prep time: 10 minutes

Total time: 25 minutes

Absolutely perfect for Kalbi. Used tamari instead of the soy sauce to keep it gluten free and mixed it in the food processor for ease in chopping the garlic and ginger.

Ingredients

- 1/4 cup green onions, chopped
- 1/4 cup garlic, minced
- 1/2 cup onion, diced
- 1 cup sesame oil
- 2 cups sugar
- 3 cups of soy sauce

Instructions

1. Mix the ingredients (this will yield almost 2 qt!).
2. Marinade about 1/2 cup per pound of beef or chicken.
3. Saute on medium high, or grill until done.
4. Keep unused portions refrigerated.

Nutritional value (per serving)

- Calories: 25
- Fat: 0g
- Protein: 0g
- Carbs: 6g

This Page Is Intentionally Left Blank

CHAPTER 10:
SIDE DISHES

MICRO HOT SAUERKRAUT CLUBS

Servings: 2

Prep time: 3 minutes

Total time: 6 minutes

This easy-to-make sauerkraut is a tasty hot dog topping. Use it to make our Classic Reubens and Pierogi with Sauerkraut and Mushrooms.

Ingredients

- 4 thick slices of French bread
- 1 tbsp butter
- 4 slices of bologna
- 4 slices of salami
- 1 (16-oz.) can of sauerkraut
- 1 cup Mozzarella cheese, shredded

Instructions

1. Spread butter on French bread and add a slice of bologna and salami.
2. Add sauerkraut and cheese.
3. Place on a microwave-safe plate and microwave for 3-4 minutes.

Nutritional value (per serving)

- Calories: 5
- Fat: 0g
- Protein: 0g
- Carbs: 1g

ROASTED ACORN SQUASH WITH PINE NUTS

Servings: 4

Prep time: 5 minutes

Total time: 15 minutes

Tender, sweet, delicious Honey Roasted Acorn Squash with Pine Nuts, a dash of cinnamon, and thyme for a hint of savory flavor. You can use olive oil instead of butter for a healthier twist.

Ingredients

- 2 tbsps unsalted butter
- 2 tbsps brown sugar
- 1 tsp sage
- 2 medium acorn sq uash, sliced into 1-inch wedges
- 2 tbsps toasted pine nuts or almonds
- salt and black pepper to taste

Instructions

1. In a microwave-safe casserole dish, melt butter.
2. Stir brown sugar and sage into butter until well combined. Add squash wedges.
3. Bake for 5-10 minutes in the microwave until squash is tender.
4. Sprinkle with nuts.

Nutritional value (per serving)

- Calories: 175
- Fat: 12g
- Protein: 2g
- Carbs: 18g

BAKED HERB POTATOES

Servings: 3

Prep time: 15 minutes

Total time: 55 minutes

While roasted potatoes are usually best fresh out the oven, they can still make great leftovers! Let them cool down completely before storing them in an air tight container in the refrigerator.

Ingredients

- 9 medium potatoes, peeled and thinly sliced
- 2 to 3 medium thinly-sliced onions
- 2 to 3 teaspoons dried basil or oregano
- 6 tablespoons melted butter

Instructions

1. Place half of the sliced potatoes and half of the sliced onions in a buttered nine-inch pie plate.
2. Sprinkle with half of the dried herbs and drizzle with one tablespoon of butter.
3. Repeat layers until you have ended with the remaining melted butter.
4. Season with salt and pepper and cover the plate with aluminum foil.
5. Bake at 425 degrees for about 20 to 25 minutes.
6. Uncover and bake for 15 to 20 minutes longer, or until the potatoes are tender.

Nutritional value (per serving)

- Calories: 344
- Fat: 9g
- Protein: 7g
- Carbs: 60g

CHIVE AND ONION CHEESY POTATOES

Servings: 2

Prep time: 5 minutes

Total time: 20 minutes

A friend once told me about a potato dish her mother used to make. She remembered that Swiss cheese and butter were standouts. Here's my re-creation—and my friend actually liked it better than her mom's version.

Ingredients

- 1(10-oz.) can of cream of celery soup
- 1 (8-oz.) package of chive and onion cream cheese
- 2 cups frozen cubed potatoes
- 1/2 cup cheddar cheese, shredded

Instructions

1. In a microwave-safe casserole dish, stir together soup and cream cheese.
2. Microwave for 2 minutes or until cream cheese is melted into the soup.
3. Fold in potatoes and combine until well covered.
4. Bake for 10 minutes in the microwave or until potatoes are tender.
5. Sprinkle with cheddar cheese and cook another 2 minutes until cheese is melted.

NB: If using fresh potatoes you'll need to cook for additional time.

Nutritional value (per serving)

- Calories: 90
- Fat: 0g
- Protein: 2g
- Carbs: 21g

BROCCOLI DELIGHT

Servings: 8

Prep time: 10 minutes

Total time: 50 minutes

It's the best thing I ever made (apparently), but no one would let me share it—until now.

Ingredients

- 40 ounces of frozen chopped broccoli
- 4 cups of cooked rice
- 2 jars (4 ounces) chopped and drained pimientos
- 2 cups finely chopped celery
- 2 cups sour cream
- 2 cans condensed cream of mushroom soup or cream of celery soup
- 1/2 teaspoon salt
- 1/2 teaspoon ground black pepper
- 1 cup shredded cheddar cheese

Instructions

1. Cook broccoli as directed on package.
2. Drain and combine with the cooked rice, pimientos, celery, sour cream, soup, salt, and pepper.
3. Transfer to a two-quart casserole dish and sprinkle cheese over the top.
4. Bake at 325 degrees for 20-30 minutes, or until thoroughly heated.

Nutritional value (per serving)

- Calories: 312
- Fat: 19g
- Protein: 7g
- Carbs: 32g

CREAMED CORN

Servings: 3

Prep time: 3 minutes

Total time: 10 minutes

Five ingredients are all you'll need for my popular creamed corn recipe. It's wonderful no matter what the occasion is. Try it on a barbecue buffet or holiday menu.

Ingredients

- 2 cups fresh or frozen corn
- 1/2 package of cream cheese
- 2 tablespoons butter or margarine
- 1 tablespoon sugar
- 1/2 teaspoon salt

Instructions

1. In a saucepan, combine all ingredients and bring to a boil.
2. Reduce heat and simmer uncovered for 6-8 minutes.

Nutritional value (per serving)

- Calories: 70
- Fat: 1g
- Protein: 1g
- Carbs: 14g

SPICY BBQ CORN

Servings: 8

Prep time: 15 minutes

Total time: 35 minutes

Who needs butter when you can have a Thai-style spicy-hot dipping sauce? And, because the husks char a bit on the outside, some of that flavor is transmitted to the kernels and you get corn that really tastes grilled.

Ingredients

- 8 ears of corn, husked and cleaned
- 1 stick of butter, melted
- 2 tbsps spicy barbecue sauce

Instructions

1. Set the grill temperature to medium high.
2. Wrap each ear of corn tightly in aluminum foil.
3. Place the wrapped corn on the grill and cook for 18 minutes, turning occasionally.
4. Remove the corn and unwrap. Place the melted butter into a small mixing bowl.
5. Whisk the barbecue sauce into the butter.
6. Use a pastry brush and brush each ear of corn with the barbecue butter mixture, making sure to cover the whole ear of corn.

Nutritional value (per serving)

- Calories: 165
- Fat: 9g
- Protein: 1g
- Carbs: 20g

MICRO COOKED MUSHROOMS PATTIES

Servings: 2

Prep time: 10 minutes

Total time: 20 minutes

If you've ever cooked mushrooms, whether frying, baking or boiling, you'll know that they start off looking dry and then produce more liquid than you'd anticipated, which means that despite their appearance they are very juicy. This makes them ideal for microwaving as you don't have to add a single extra ingredient if you don't want to. Do make sure you eat the juices as well to get the maximum amount of nutrients.

Ingredients

- ¼ cups of cornstarch
- 2½ cups beef broth
- 1 (6-oz.) jar of sliced mushrooms
- 4 tsps Worcestershire sauce
- 1 tsp dried bail
- 1 egg
- 1/2 cup breadcrumbs
- 1 onion, grated
- 1/2 tsp seasoning salt
- 1/4 tsp pepper
- 1/2 lbs ground beef

Instructions

1. Blend together cornstarch and beef broth in a microwave-safe casserole dish.
2. Stir in mushrooms, Worcestershire sauce, and basil.
3. In a separate bowl, mix together egg, bread crumbs, onion, salt, and pepper.
4. Add ground beef to breadcrumb mixture.
5. Mix together until you can form it into 6 patties and place them in the microwave-safe casserole dish.
6. Microwave patties on high for 6-10 minutes or until patties are cooked through.
7. Halfway through cooking, turn patties around.

Nutritional value (per serving)

- Calories: 15
- Fat: 0.2g
- Protein: 2.2g
- Carbs: 2.3g

LASAGNA IN A MUG

Servings: 1

Prep time: 10 minutes

Total time: 25 minutes

This single serving pasta bowl cooks in the microwave and is ready in less than 15 minutes! So this isn't your traditional layered lasagna. But it does consist of lasagna noodles, tomatoes, and cheese. And it tastes pretty darn good.

Ingredients

- 2 pasta lasagna sheets, ready to serve
- 6 oz. of water
- 1 teaspoon olive oil or cooking spray
- 3 tablespoons pizza sauce
- 4 tablespoons ricotta or cottage cheese
- 3 tablespoons spinach
- 1 tablespoon cheddar cheese
- 2 tablespoons cooked sausage (optional)

Instructions

1. Break lasagna sheets and place properly inside the mug.
2. Spray with olive oil to avoid sticking. Cover lasagna with water.
3. Cook for 3-4 minutes in microwave oven or until pasta looks tender.
4. Remove the water and set pasta aside.
5. In the same mug, add pizza sauce and place a few pieces of pasta in the mug.
6. Add spinach, ricotta, and sausage in layers. Sprinkle cheddar cheese on top.
7. Continue layers again, starting with pasta.
8. Place in microwave and cover with a microwave-safe cover or paper towel to avoid splatters.
9. Cook in microwave oven for 3 minutes or until lasagna is heated through.
10. Let cool for 1-2 minutes and enjoy the taste.

Nutritional value (per serving)

- Calories: 478
- Fat: 38g
- Protein: 24g
- Carbs: 10g

BROCCOLI CHEESE SOUP

Servings: 4

Prep time: 10 minutes

Total time: 20 minutes

You'd think that it was made with heavy cream based on how thick, rich, and truly decadent it tastes.

Ingredients

- 10-oz. package of frozen broccoli
- 2 cups milk
- 1/3 cup flour
- 1 cup water
- 2 cups Velvetta cheese cut into cubes
- 1 cup half and half
- 2 chicken bouillon cubes**nstructions**

1. Combine milk, flour, water, chicken bouillon cubes, and half and half in a microwave-safe dish.
2. Whisk together and then add in broccoli and cook in the microwave for several minutes, stirring often.
3. Stir in cheese and cook until cheese is melted and broccoli is tender.

Nutritional value (per serving)

- Calories: 240
- Fat: 20g
- Protein: 9g
- Carbs: 5g

This Page Is Intentionally Left Blank

CHAPTER 11:
DRINK RECIPES

STRAWBERRY MILKSHAKE

Servings: 2

Prep time: 25 minutes

Total time: 25 minutes

Creamy, frothy, sweet, and icy cold, milkshakes can cool you off on a hot and humid day or satisfy an ice cream urge in a unique way.

Ingredients

- 1/2 pound fresh strawberries
- 1 tablespoon sugar
- 1 teaspoon vanilla extract
- 1 pint vanilla ice cream
- 1/2 cup milk
- small whole strawberries (garnish)

Instructions

1. Cut the tops off of the strawberries and slice them into pieces.
2. In a medium bowl, combine the sliced strawberries, sugar, and vanilla extract. Stir to combine.
3. Set aside and allow to sit for at least 20 minutes and for up to 1 hour.
4. Place the strawberries with any juices, ice cream, and milk in a blender. Blend until smooth.
5. Pour into large glasses and, if desired, put a strawberry on the rim of each glass.

Nutritional value (per serving)

- Calories: 613
- Fat: 49g
- Protein: 10g
- Carbs: 39g

LEMONADE FOR KIDS

Servings: 6

Prep time: 20 minutes

Total time: 25 minutes

Once you try this lemonade recipe, you'll never go back to bottled or powdered lemonade again.

Feel free to adjust the sweetness of this lemonade recipe by adding more or less sugar to suit your taste. A sprig of fresh mint makes the perfect garnish.

Ingredients

- 1 ¼ cups sugar (granulated)
- 6 cups water (cold; divided)
- 5 to 8 lemons
- lemon slices or fresh mint (garnish)

Instructions

1. In a medium (2 or 3-quart) saucepan, combine the sugar and 1 cup of water.
2. Bring to a boil over medium heat, stirring until all the sugar is dissolved.
3. Remove from heat and cool to room temperature.
4. Refrigerate this mixture (simple syrup) while you make the rest of the lemonade.
5. Juice the lemons over a strainer, until you have 1 cup of fresh lemon juice.
6. In a pitcher, add the lemon juice to the remaining 5 cups of cold water.
7. Stir in the refrigerated simple syrup.
8. Serve in ice-filled glasses, garnishing with lemon slices or fresh mint, and enjoy.

Nutritional value (per serving)

- Calories: 184
- Fat: 0g
- Protein: 1g
- Carbs: 49g

ORANGE CREAMSICLE SMOOTHIES

Servings: 2

Prep time: 5 minutes

Total time: 3 hours 5 minutes

These refreshing orange creamsicle smoothies taste just like the ice cream bar, but they're healthy enough to serve for breakfast.

Ingredients

- 1 (11-ounce) can mandarin oranges in juice
- 1/2 cup pineapple (frozen chunks)
- 1/2 cup yogurt (vanilla, or vanilla soy yogurt)
- 1 tablespoon honey
- 1 cup soy milk (vanilla)

Instructions

1. Open the can of oranges and drain.
2. Place in a zip-top plastic bag and freeze for several hours.
3. Place the frozen oranges and pineapple chunks in the bottom of a blender or food processor.
4. Add the remaining ingredients in the order listed.
5. Puree until the mixture reaches the texture of a milkshake.
6. Add more ice, if desired, until an icy consistency is achieved.
7. Serve and enjoy!

Nutritional value (per serving)

- Calories: 215
- Fat: 3g
- Protein: 6g
- Carbs: 44g

CREAMY AND RICH WATERMELON SMOOTHIE

Servings: 3

Prep time: 10 minutes

Total time: 70 minutes

Because watermelons have that extremely high water content, the best way of ensuring a thick and creamy smoothie is to freeze the fruit beforehand.

Ingredients

- 1 medium seedless watermelon (or 3 cups frozen fruit for this recipe)
- 1 cup almond milk
- (or soy milk, or whole milk)
- 1/2 cup vanilla yogurt
- 3 tablespoons maple syrup
- 2 small wedges of watermelon
- 2 sprigs ofmint (garnish)

Instructions

1. Cut the watermelon into small chunks of about ½ inch square.
2. Reserve a few wedges, rind included, for the garnish. Line a cookie sheet with baking paper.
3. Place the fresh-cut watermelon on the cookie sheet, leaving space between the pieces.
4. Cover with plastic wrap and freeze for 1 hour.
5. Once frozen, measure 3 cups of frozen watermelon and place in a blender.
6. Top the fruit with milk, yogurt, and maple syrup. Blend until smooth.
7. Serve the watermelon smoothies immediately in chilled glasses.
8. Garnish with a wedge of watermelon and fresh mint, if desired.

Nutritional value (per serving)

- Calories: 14
- Fat: 1g
- Protein: 3g
- Carbs: 33g

PEANUT BUTTER BANANA SMOOTHIES

Servings: 12

Prep time: 10 minutes

Total time: 10 minutes

If you don't have time to freeze the banana slices in advance, just use regular bananas and add more ice. And if you like, you can substitute regular milk (whole or low-fat), almond milk, or even coconut milk for the soy milk in this recipe.

Ingredients

- 2 cups frozen banana slices (approximately 2 medium bananas)
- 1 cup frozen pineapple chunks
- 1 cup ice
- 1 1/2 cups vanilla soy milk
- 1/4 cup peanut butter
- 1/4 cup vanilla yogurt
- 2 tbsps honey

Instructions

1. Place frozen banana slices, frozen pineapple chunks, and ice in the bottom of a blender.
2. Pour soy milk over fruit. Add remaining ingredients. Purée until smooth.
3. If the blender doesn't seem to be crushing the pineapple chunks well enough, stop it.
4. Push the pineapple down with a spoon. Restart.
5. Garnish with chopped roasted peanuts, if desired, and serve immediately.

Nutritional value (per serving)

- Calories: 401
- Fat: 13g
- Protein: 10g
- Carbs: 69g

NO SUGAR FROZEN STRAWBERRY LEMONADE

Servings: 2

Prep time: 3 minutes

Total time: 3 minutes

Ingredients

- 1/2 cup lemon juice
- 1/4 cup water
- 1 teaspoon lemon li uid stevia
- 1/2 cup Swerve sweetener
- 1/2 cup strawberries
- Pinch salt
- 2 cups ice

Instructions

1. Add lemon juice, water, liquid stevia, and Swerve to your high-powered blender.
2. Remove the stem of the strawberries, wash them, and then add them to the blender.
3. Give the blender a quick whir then add ice.
4. Continue to blend until ice is thoroughly incorporated and lemonade is thick and slushy.
5. Taste and adjust sweetness if needed.
6. Serve in your favorite glass and enjoy!

Nutritional value (per serving)

- Calories: 36
- Fat: 0g
- Protein: 1g
- Carbs: 10g

MANGO JULIUS MOCKTAIL

Servings: 1

Prep time: 5 minutes

Total time: 5 minutes

Many of us have childhood memories of enjoying this delicious frozen smoothie treat –
it is a wonderfully blended drink that is great in summer or anytime you have a craving
for a more innocent mocktail.

Ingredients

- 1 cup of fresh or frozen mango juice
- 2 ounces 2% milk
- 1 teaspoon vanilla extract
- 2 tablespoons sugar
- 1 scoop of vanilla ice cream

Instructions

1. Place all ingredients in a blender with 1/2 cup of ice.
2. Blend until smooth.
3. Pour into a chilled hurricane glass.

Nutritional value (per serving)

- Calories: 352
- Fat: 9g
- Protein: 4g
- Carbs: 64g

LOW-CALORIE BLUEBERRY SMOOTHIE

Servings: 1

Prep time: 5 minutes

Total time: 5 minutes

Ingredients

- 6 ounces low-fat blueberry yogurt (2/3 cup)
- 1/2 cup ice
- 1/4 cup fresh or frozen blueberries
- handful blueberries (garnish)

Instructions

1. Add the blueberry yogurt, ice cubes, and blueberries to a blender.
2. Blend on high until the ice cubes are crushed and you have a smooth consistency.
3. Pour into a glass and serve immediately, garnished with a few extra blueberries if desired.

Nutritional value (per serving)

- Calories: 197
- Fat: 2g
- Protein: 7g
- Carbs: 39g

STRAWBERRY LIME SMOOTHIES

Servings: 3

Prep time: 5 minutes

Total time: 5 minutes

Ingredients:

- 1 cup strawberry yogurt
- 1/2 cup 2% milk
- 2 to 4 tablespoons lime juice
- 2 tablespoons honey
- 1/4 teaspoon ground cinnamon
- 2 cups fresh strawberries, hulled

Instructions

1. Process all ingredients in a covered blender until smooth.

Nutritional value (per serving)

- Calories: 181
- Fat: 2g
- Protein: 5g
- Carbs: 38g

OREO MILKSHAKE

Servings: 2

Prep time: 5 minutes

Total time: 5 minutes

With a bit of cookie crunch, rich chocolate sauce, and creamy texture, it's no wonder that people are so fond of this flavorful Oreo milkshake. Serve with a colorful straw.

Ingredients

- 1 pint vanilla ice cream
- 1 cup milk (preferably whole milk)
- 8 Oreo cookies (or other chocolate sandwich cookies)
- 1 tablespoon chocolate sauce
- 2 Oreo cookies (garnish)

Instructions

1. Place the vanilla ice cream, milk, 8 Oreo cookies, and the chocolate sauce in a blender.
2. Puree until smooth. Pour the milkshakes into two tall glasses.
3. Top each with crushed Oreo cookie crumbs.
4. Enjoy!

Nutritional value (per serving)

- Calories: 790
- Fat: 33g
- Protein: 17g
- Carbs: 111g

PUMPKIN PIE SMOOTHIES

Servings: 4

Prep time: 10 minutes

Total time: 10 minutes

Ingredients:

- 1 can (15 ounces) pumpkin, chilled
- 1½ cups evaporated milk (about 10 ounces), chilled
- 1 cup orange juice
- 1/3 cup packed brown sugar
- 1/2 teaspoon pumpkin pie spice
- 1/4 teaspoon ground cinnamon
- 1 small ripe banana, cut into thirds

Instructions

1. Process all ingredients in a blender until smooth.

Nutritional value (per serving)

- Calories: 256
- Fat: 6g
- Protein: 7g
- Carbs: 46g

EGG CREAM

Servings: 1

Prep time: 2 minutes

Total time: 2 minutes

The irony of the egg cream is that it contains neither eggs, nor cream. How this classic beverage got its name and even how it was invented in the first place is a subject of much debate.

Ingredients

- 1 cup milk (cold)
- 1/4 cup seltzer water (cold)
- 2 tablespoons chocolate-flavored syrup

Instructions

1. Place a 12-ounce serving glass in the freezer to chill.
2. Pour the cold milk into the chilled glass.
3. Pour the seltzer into the glass until the white head reaches the top of the glass.
4. Spoon the syrup into the glass and stir to combine.
5. Serve with a straw.

Nutritional value (per serving)

- Calories: 119
- Fat: 3g
- Protein: 3g
- Carbs: 20g

This Page Is Intentionally Left Blank

CHAPTER 12:

DESSERT RECIPES

MICROWAVE MINI CHOCOLATE CAKE

Servings: 1

Prep time: 10 minutes

Total time: 20 minutes

Ingredients

- 4 tablespoons all-purpose flour
- 4 tablespoons sugar
- 2 tablespoons unsweetened cocoa
- 1 egg
- 3 tablespoons milk
- 3 tablespoons vegetable oil
- a handful of chocolate chips

Instructions

1. Spray a microwave-safe large coffee cup with cooking spray.
2. Add flour, then sugar, and cocoa inside the coffee mug.
3. Blend dry ingredients together. Add milk, oil, and 1 egg.
4. Sprinkle chocolate chips on top. Gently stir until well combined.
5. Place in microwave and cook for 3 minutes.
6. If desired, add a scoop of ice cream or whipped cream and sprinkle with chocolate chips
7. Top with strawberries.

Nutritional value (per serving)

- Calories: 174
- Fat: 4g
- Protein: 4g
- Carbs: 32g

RASPBERRY ICE CREAM IN A BAG

Servings: 4

Prep time: 10 minutes

Total time: 15 minutes

Ingredients:

- 1 cup half-and-half cream
- 1/2 cup fresh raspberries
- 1/4 cup sugar
- 2 tablespoons evaporated milk
- 1 teaspoon vanilla extract
- 4 cups coarsely crushed ice
- 3/4 cup salt

Instructions

1. Using two 1-quart resealable plastic bags, place 1 bag inside the other.
2. Place the first 5 ingredients inside the inner bag.
3. Seal both bags, pressing out as much air as possible.
4. Place the 2 bags in a gallon-size resealable plastic freezer bag.
5. Add ice and salt. Seal the freezer bag, again pressing out as much air as possible.
6. Shake and knead cream mixture until thickened, about 5 minutes.

Nutritional value (per serving)

- Calories: 299
- Fat: 13g
- Protein: 5g
- Carbs: 35g

NO-BAKE PEANUT BUTTER TREATS

Servings: 15

Prep time: 10 minutes

Total time: 10 minutes

Ingredients:

- 1/3 cup chunky peanut butter
- 1/4 cup honey
- 1/2 teaspoon vanilla extract
- 1/3 cup nonfat dry milk powder
- 1/3 cup quick-cooking oats
- 2 tablespoons graham cracker crumbs

Instructions

1. In a small bowl, combine the peanut butter, honey, and vanilla.
2. Stir in the milk powder, oats, and graham cracker crumbs.
3. Shape into 1-inch balls.
4. Cover and refrigerate until serving.

Test Kitchen tips

1. Let peanut butter be the star in no bake Christmas treats like this.
2. Or for additional cookie ideas see the favorite cookies in America, state-by-state.

Nutritional value (per serving)

- Calories: 70
- Fat: 3g
- Protein: 3g
- Carbs: 9g

BASIC VANILLA CAKE

Servings: 6

Prep time: 10 minutes

Total time: 50 minutes

This simple vanilla cake is the perfect cake for kids to bake.

Ingredients

- 4 ½ ounces of butter, softened
- 1 1/2 cups sugar
- 2 eggs
- 1 cup of plain flour
- 1 cup of self-raising flour
- (or 2 cups of plain flour and 2 tsp baking soda)
- 1 1/2 teaspons of vanilla extract
- 1 cup milk

Instructions

1. Preheat your oven to 356°F and line and grease a 9-inch cake tin
2. In a large bowl, combine the butter and sugar and beat until light and fluffy
3. Add the eggs and vanilla, and mix well.
4. Add the flour and milk alternately, mixing well until combined.
5. Pour the mixture into your prepared cake tin
6. Bake for 40 minutes or until a skewer inserted comes out clean.
7. When cool, ice the cake with a basic mixture of icing sugar and milk and cover with sprinkles.

Nutritional value (per serving)

- Calories: 185
- Fat: 8g
- Protein: 2.5g
- Carbs: 26g

EASY CAKE MIX BARS

Servings: 3 dozen

Prep time: 5 minutes

Total time: 50 minutes

They're so easy to eat, easy to make, and easy on the wallet.

Ingredients

- 1 package of yellow cake mix (regular size)
- 1 large egg
- 1/2 cup 2% milk
- 1/3 cup canola oil
- 1 cup white baking chips
- 1/3 cup jimmies

Instructions

1. Preheat oven to 350°.
2. In a large bowl, combine cake mix, egg, milk, and oil (mixture will be thick).
3. Stir in baking chips and jimmies. Spread into a greased 15x10x1-inch baking pan.
4. Bake 18-20 minutes or until a toothpick inserted in the center comes out clean.
5. Cool completely in pan on a wire rack. Cut into bars.
6. Freeze option: freeze bars in freezer containers.
7. To use, thaw in covered containers before serving.

Nutritional value (per serving)

- Calories: 113
- Fat: 5g
- Protein: 1g
- Carbs: 16g

BASIC BANANA MUFFINS

Servings: 1 dozen

Prep time: 10 minutes

Total time: 30 minutes

Not only are these banana bread muffins like cupcakes, but they're ready, start to finish, in just half an hour!

Ingredients

- 1 ½ cups all-purpose flour
- 1 cup sugar
- 1 teaspoon baking soda
- 1/2 teaspoon salt
- 3 medium-ripe bananas
- 1 large egg, room temperature
- 1/3 cup vegetable oil
- 1 teaspoon vanilla extract

Instructions

1. In a large bowl, combine dry ingredients. In another bowl, mash the bananas.
2. Add egg, oil, and vanilla to banana; mix well. Stir into the dry ingredients just until moistened.
3. Fill greased or paper-lined muffin cups half full.
4. Bake at 375° for 18-22 minutes or until a toothpick inserted in the center comes out clean.
5. Cool for 10 minutes; remove from pan to a wire rack to cool completely.

Nutritional value (per serving)

- Calories: 209
- Fat: 7g
- Protein: 2g
- Carbs: 36g

ROOT BEER FLOAT CAKE

Servings: 15

Prep time: 15 minutes

Total time: 45 minutes

Add root beer to both the cake batter and fluffy frosting of this summery dessert to get that great root beer float taste. Serve this moist cake to a bunch of hungry kids and watch it disappear!

Ingredients

- 1 package white cake mix (regular size)
- 1¾ cups cold root beer, divided
- 1/4 cup canola oil
- 2 large eggs
- 1 envelope whipped topping mix (Dream Whip)

Instructions

1. In a large bowl, combine cake mix, 1 ¼ cups root beer, oil, and eggs.
2. Beat on low speed for 2 minutes or stir by hand for 3 minutes.
3. Pour into a greased 13x9-in. baking pan.
4. Bake at 350° for 30-35 minutes. Cool completely on a wire rack.
5. In a small bowl, combine the whipped topping mix and remaining root beer.
6. Beat until soft peaks form. Frost cake.
7. Store in the refrigerator.

Nutritional value (per serving)

- Calories: 203
- Fat: 8g
- Protein: 2g
- Carbs: 31g

FUDGY MINT COOKIES

Servings: 3 dozen

Prep time: 15 minutes

Total time: 25 minutes

Chocolate lovers will get a double dose when they bite into this cake-like cookie. The cookies are especially popular served alongside a big scoop of mint chocolate chip ice cream!

Ingredients

- 1 package devil's food cake mix (regular size)
- 1/2 cup butter, softened
- 2 large eggs, room temperature
- 1 tablespoon water
- 2 tablespoons confectioners' sugar
- 2 packages (5 ounces each) chocolate-covered thin mint candies

Instructions

1. Preheat oven to 375°.
2. In a large bowl, mix cake mix, butter, eggs, and water to form a soft dough.
3. Shape dough into 1-inch balls; roll in confectioners' sugar.
4. Place 2 inches apart on ungreased baking sheets. Bake until set, 8-10 minutes.
5. Immediately press a mint into the center of each cookie.
6. Cool on pans 2 minutes. Remove from pans to wire racks to cool.

Nutritional value (per serving)

- Calories: 102
- Fat: 4g
- Protein: 1g
- Carbs: 16g

CHOCOLATE LOVER'S PIZZA

Servings: 16

Prep time: 10 minutes

Total time: 20 minutes

I created this after my Dad said that my graham cracker crust should be topped with dark chocolate and pecans. It's easy to customize by adding your favorite chocolate and toppers. My Dad thinks the whole world should know about this pizza!

Ingredients

- 2 ½ cups graham cracker crumbs
- 2/3 cup butter, melted
- 1/2 cup sugar
- 2 packages Dove dark chocolate candies (9 ½ ounces each)
- 1/2 cup chopped pecans

Instructions

1. Combine the cracker crumbs, butter, and sugar; press onto a greased 12-inch pizza pan.
2. Bake at 375° for 7-9 minutes or until lightly browned.
3. Top with chocolate candies; bake for 2-3 minutes longer or until chocolate is softened.
4. Spread chocolate over crust; sprinkle with nuts. Cool on a wire rack for 15 minutes.
5. Refrigerate for 1-2 hours or until set.

Nutritional value (per serving)

- Calories: 349
- Fat: 23g
- Protein: 3g
- Carbs: 37g

PEANUT BUTTER KISS COOKIES

Servings: 2 ½ dozens

Prep time: 20 minutes

Total time: 10 minutes

Baking peanut butter kiss cookies to share doesn't get much easier than this. Stir together four ingredients. Bake. Top with a kiss. Done!

Ingredients

- 1 cup peanut butter
- 1 cup sugar
- 1 large egg, room temperature
- 1 teaspoon vanilla extract
- 30 milk chocolate kisses

Instructions

1. Preheat oven to 350°.
2. Cream peanut butter and sugar until light and fluffy. Beat in egg and vanilla.
3. Roll into 1¼-inch balls. Place 2 inches apart on ungreased baking sheets.
4. Bake until tops are slightly cracked, 10-12 minutes.
5. Immediately press 1 chocolate kiss into center of each cookie.
6. Cool for 5 minutes before removing from pans to wire racks.

Nutritional value (per serving)

- Calories: 102
- Fat: 6g
- Protein: 2g
- Carbs: 11g

CHOCOLATE MILKSHAKE

Servings: 2

Prep time: 5 minutes

Total time: 5 minutes

Nothing beats a creamy, thick chocolate shake alongside a nice burger and fries. But you don't have to go to a fast-food joint to get a great milkshake. With only three ingredients (milk, ice cream, and chocolate syrup) our chocolate milkshake is an exceptional treat, topped with a nice dollop of whipped cream.

Ingredients

- 2 cups vanilla ice cream
- 1/4 cup chocolate syrup
- 1/2 cup whole milk (cold)
- whipped cream, shaved chocolate (for garnish)
- 1/4 cup chocolate chips (optional)

Instructions

1. Place the ice cream, milk, and chocolate syrup into the blender.
2. If using chocolate chips, add those as well.
3. Blend the ingredients until completely smooth.
4. Pour into your glasses immediately, top with whipped cream
5. Decorate with shaved chocolate and Enjoy!

Nutritional value (per serving)

- Calories: 210
- Fat: 6g
- Protein: 5.6g
- Carbs: 34g

INDIVIDUAL PUDDING DIRT CUPS

Servings: 10

Prep time: 15 minutes

Total time: 1 hour 20 minutes

Use our dirt dessert as treats for Halloween parties, birthday celebrations, or kids' play dates. For larger groups, or for a different presentation, try our dirt cake instead.

Ingredients

- 2 cups milk (cold)
- 3 (10-ounces) instant chocolate pudding
- 8 ounces whipped topping (frozen)
- 1 ½ cups chocolate cookies (sandwich cookies, such as Oreos, about 16, crushed, divided)
- 20 gummy worms (for garnish)

Instructions

1. Whisk together the milk and instant pudding for 2 minutes.
2. Let stand 5 minutes to thicken.
3. Stir in frozen whipped topping and ½ cup of the crushed cookies.
4. Spoon into 10 individual cups.
5. Sprinkle remaining crushed cookies over the pudding mixture.
6. Top each cup with 2 gummy worms.
7. Chill for at least 60 minutes.
8. Enjoy.

Nutritional value (per serving)

- Calories: 366
- Fat: 18g
- Protein: 4g
- Carbs: 48g

MINI BROWNIE BITES

Servings: 24

Prep time: 10 minutes

Total time: 45 minutes

This is a great recipe to bake with kids, so have them help you top each bite with melted chocolate chips and sprinkles (snacking on a few in the process is highly encouraged).

Ingredients

- 1 package (16 oz) refrigerated chocolate fudge brownies
- 1/4 cup semisweet chocolate chips
- Multicolored sprinkles, if desired

Instructions

1. Heat oven to 350°F (325°F for nonstick pan).
2. Place paper baking cups in 24 miniature muffin cups.
3. With a sharp knife, cut each brownie dough round in half to make 2 halves; roll into balls. Place 1 ball into each muffin cup.
4. Bake 15 to 17 minutes or until toothpick inserted into center comes out almost clean.
5. Cool 10 minutes in pan; carefully remove to cooling rack.
6. In a small microwavable bowl, microwave chocolate chips uncovered on high 30 to 60 seconds, stirring after 30 seconds, until chips are melted and smooth.
7. Transfer melted chips to a small resealable food-storage plastic bag
8. Cut a small corner off on one end of the bag. Drizzle chocolate onto brownies, and top with sprinkles; serve.
9. If desired, refrigerate about 15 minutes or until chocolate drizzle is set before serving.

Nutritional value (per serving)

- Calories: 90
- Fat: 3.5g
- Protein: 1g
- Carbs: 13g

APPLE MUFFINS WITH STRAWBERRIES

Servings: 6

Prep time: 10 minutes

Total time: 30 minutes

These no-junk muffins are delicious! Sweetened with apples and a dash of maple syrup and easy on the saturated fat in favour of oil, they're a healthy alternative to the average muffin, making them perfect for kids.

Ingredients

- 1 apple peeled and grated
- 1 1/2 large eggs
- 50 g (1.8 oz) self-raising flour
- 1 tsp cinnamon
- 1 tbsp maple syrup
- 45 ml (1.4 floz) sunflower oil
- 25 g (0.9 oz) dried strawberry pieces

Instructions

1. Preheat your oven to 392°F (356°F fan-assisted), gas mark 6, 400F.
2. Put the grated apples in a large bowl with the eggs, maple syrup, and oil. Mix.
3. Add the self-raising flour and cinnamon. Mix again.
4. Add the strawberries and fold through.
5. Spoon the batter into a lightly oiled, greaseproof 12-hole muffin tin.
6. Bake for 15-20 minutes, until golden and cooked in the centre.
7. Stick a skewer in the center of a muffin to check they are cooked.

Nutritional value (per serving)

- Calories: 154
- Fat: 9g
- Protein: 3g
- Carbs: 16g

CONCLUSION

Congratulations and thank you for making it to the end of this book.

Bear in mind that it takes time to master the art of cooking and become a renowned chef.

Bringing up a child who can enjoy a cantaloupe as much as a cupcake takes patience and persistence, but it does not have to feel like a chore.

Cooking with kids doesn't have to take a lot of time and work. Whether you have toddlers or teens, your kids will love getting creative in the kitchen. And this is not only fun and cheap, but also great for giving them some life-skills, boosting their confidence, and even practicing some fine-motor skills.

Even better, helping in the kitchen can entice even the fussiest of eaters to try something new and maybe add a new veg or two to their limited repertoire.

Also, it is imperative to remind you to stick to simple recipes with your kids and read through the recipe instructions together. Take the recipe a task at a time so they don't get too overloaded with information.

In each of the recipes above, I have outlined a list of tasks that I think are appropriate for both toddlers and kids to do in the kitchen. This section is usually at the bottom of the post before the recipe card.

These tasks are, however, just a guideline.

Normally, kids' skills are all over the place when it comes to cooking – some kids will have mastered basic culinary tasks at an early age, while others will only want to sit on the counter, make a mess, and eat butter.

It's all about exposure, so meet your kiddo where they are and remember to have fun!

ABOUT THE AUTHOR

Don Perterson is a nationally recognized registered dietitian nutritionist, cooking expert, and motivational speaker inspiring millions of people to eat and live well.

He is known for developing segments for television, writing recipe cookbooks, blog posts, and he is known for his work as a spokesperson to leading great-minded people and companies nationwide.

Don has conducted more than 1,000 media interviews over the past decade, including guest appearances on *The TODAY Show*, *The Doctors*, *ABC News*, *Fox News Channel* and *CNN*. He has also written for and been interviewed by magazines such as *O*, *Shape*, *Fitness*, *Glamour*, *Parenting*, *Men's Health*, *Redbook* and *Good Housekeeping*.

In addition to his nutrition expertise, Mr. Peterson received a professional chef certificate from The New School of Cooking in Los Angeles. He enjoys using his culinary skills to develop recipes, shoot cooking videos, and teach clients how to make changes in their lives starting in the kitchen.

He graduated from the University of Delaware with a Bachelor of Science in nutrition and dietetics and completed his dietetic training at the National Institutes of Health in Bethesda, Maryland. Don received a Masters of Science in nutrition communication from the Friedman School of Nutrition Science and Policy at Tufts University in Boston, Massachusetts.

When he's not traveling the world talking about nutrition and cooking, you can find Don at home in Los Angeles with his wife and two children.

INDEX

A

APPLE MUFFINS WITH STRAWBERRIES

B

BACON BREAKFAST PIZZA

BACON GRILLED CHEESE

BAKED HERB POTATOES

BASIC BANANA MUFFINS

BASIC PANCAKES

BASIC VANILLA CAKE

BBQ CHICKEN

BLT WRAPS

BROCCOLI CHEESE SOUP

BROCCOLI DELIGHT

C

CHEDDAR CORN DOG MUFFINS

CHEESE FRIES

CHEESY QUESADILLAS

CHICKEN & BACON ROLL-UPS

CHICKEN AND PEA CASSEROLE

CHICKEN MEATBALL SOUP

CHICKEN PHILLY CHEESESTEAK

CHICKEN RICE SOUP

CHILI MAC SUPPER

CHIVE AND ONION CHEESY POTATOES

CHOCOLATE CHIP, PB & BANANA SANDWICHES

CHOCOLATE LOVER'S PIZZA

CHOCOLATE MILKSHAKE

COPYCAT CHICKEN SALAD

CREAMED CORN

CREAMY AND RICH WATERMELON SMOOTHIE

CREAMY BEEF NOODLES

CREAMY CHICKEN ALFREDO

CREAMY TUNA SKILLET

D

E

EASY CAKE MIX BARS

EASY HOMEMADE CHICKEN NOODLE SOUP

EASY KETO CHEESY BACON

EASY KOREAN BBQ MARINADE

EGG CREAM

F

FRESH STRAWBERRY BREAKFAST TACOS

FRUITY CHICKEN SALAD PITAS

FRUITY PEANUT BUTTER PITAS

FUDGY MINT COOKIES

G

GARLIC BREAD PIZZA SANDWICHES

GARLIC TOAST PIZZAS

GLAZED DOUGHNUT HOLES

GRANOLA TRAIL MIX

GRILLED HUMMUS TURKEY SANDWICH

H

HAM BEAN SOUP

HAM, MACARONI, AND CHEESE CHOWDER

HOMEMADE HAM, TURKEY, AND CHEESE POCKETS

I

INDIVIDUAL PUDDING DIRT CUPS

INDONESIAN CHICKEN SATAY

J

K

KIDDIE CRUNCH MIX

L

LASAGNA IN A MUG

LEMONADE FOR KIDS

LEMON-APRICOT FRUIT POPS

LIFE-CHANGING SOFT SCRAMBLED EGGS

LOADED BAKED POTATO DIP

LOW-CALORIE BLUEBERRY SMOOTHIE

LUNCH BOX PIZZAS

M

MAKING AN OMELETTE

MANGO JULIUS MOCKTAIL

MANGO MONDAY MEAT LOAF

MARSHMALLOW FRUIT DIP

MICRO COOKED MUSHROOMS PATTIES

MICRO HOT SAUERKRAUT CLUBS

MICROWAVE MINI CHOCOLATE CAKE

MINI BROWNIE BITES

N

NO-BAKE PEANUT BUTTER TREATS

NO SUGAR FROZEN STRAWBERRY LEMONADE

O

ORANGE CREAMSICLE SMOOTHIES

OREO MILKSHAKE

P

PBJ ON A STICK

PEANUT BUTTER BANANA SMOOTHIES

PEANUT BUTTER GRANOLA PINWHEELS

PEANUT BUTTER KISS COOKIES

PEANUT BUTTER OATMEAL

PIZZA SOUP

POTATO CHICKEN CASSEROLE

PRINCESS TOAST

PUMPKIN PIE SMOOTHIES

Q

R

RAINBOW SPAGHETTI

RANCH SNACK MIX

RASPBERRY ICE CREAM IN A BAG

RISE AND SHINE PARFAIT

ROASTED ACORN SQUASH WITH PINE NUTS

ROOT BEER FLOAT CAKE

ROTISSERIE CHICKEN PANINI

S

SCRAMBLED EGG TOAST

SKILLET PIZZA

SOUTHERN SALMON STEW

SPAGHETTI CUPCAKES

SPICY BBQ CORN

STRAWBERRY LIME SMOOTHIES

STRAWBERRY MILKSHAKE

SWEET AND SOUR CHICKEN

T

TEXAS TUMBLEWEEDS

TRADITIONAL TUNA SALAD

TURKEY RANCH WRAPS

TURKEY WAFFLEWICHES

U

V

W

X

Y

YOGURT & HONEY FRUIT CUPS

YOGURT PARFAIT

Z

Made in the USA
Las Vegas, NV
29 October 2022

58132532R00146